Cookie —— School

Cookie —— School

Recipes, Tips
and Techniques
for Perfectly
Baked Treats

Amanda Powell

Creator of A Cookie Named Desire

PAGE STREET
PUBLISHING CO.

PAGE STREET
PUBLISHING CO.

First published in 2023 by

Page Street Publishing Co.

27 Congress Street, Suite 1511

Salem, MA 01970

www.pagestreetpublishing.com

Distributed by Macmillan, sales in Canada by The Canadian Manda Group.

27   26   25   24   23   1   2   3   4   5

ISBN-13: 978-1-64567-779-6

ISBN-10: 1-64567-779-6

Library of Congress Control Number: 2022948027

Cover and book design by Laura Benton for Page Street Publishing Co.

Photography by Amanda Powell

Printed and bound in the United States of America

This cookbook is dedicated to my late fiancé, Quinlin Tempest, a.k.a. Timothy Bridgeman. You were my biggest supporter and my best friend. You are the reason this book exists. I love you endlessly.

This book is also dedicated to my favorite human in the world, my child, Nadia. You are my everything. My inspiration. My heart.

Table of Contents

Introduction

I'm pretty sure the contentment and satisfaction you get when biting into a freshly baked cookie still warm from the oven is one that is universally recognized. For all the ease and convenience of store-bought cookies, nothing beats the aroma, texture and flavor of a homemade cookie. You remember the cookies you bake more than the trips to the store to buy cookies long after they're gone.

A new baker might be able to make a delicious cookie with a solid recipe, even if it doesn't turn out exactly as they pictured it. But when we want to get experimental and really test the limits of our imagination, it can get a little tricky, and we might end up with pools of cookie dough that refuse to bake up or hard, crumbly balls that fall apart before we even get them in the oven.

This leaves us feeling frustrated, defeated and angry at all the wasted time and ingredients that ended up in the trash. I can't count the number of times this was and still is a big part of my life. But through the mistakes and, with a bit of basic baking science know-how, I've come to embrace the mess and use it to learn how to adjust recipes to fit anything my imagination wants to try.

That is why I wanted to write this book. I spent years learning how to perfect all my favorite cookies, many of which you can also find on my website, A Cookie Named Desire. I eventually took my passion for baking and recipe development further by pursuing higher education in food science. And now, I want to take what I've learned and share it with anyone else who constantly craves the perfect cookie, but maybe felt they were no good in the kitchen. I am here to not just tell you, but to show you that you are.

I believe anyone can not only bake a delicious cookie, they can take easy tips and tricks to understand how to change up a recipe to match what they imagined. This book is meant to be like a fun and delicious student guide taking you from the easy Freshman-level cookies all the way to the advanced Senior cookies. We will work through such basics as how to make your perfect chocolate chip cookie and learn how to make fun recipes, such as Magical Peanut Butter S'mores and Sweetheart Red Velvet Sandwiches. Finally, we will tackle and master the elusive macaron.

I hope for this book to be more than just a cookbook. I want to give you the tools, information and inspiration to use these recipes as a template and canvas for creating your own cookie recipes. Recipe development will always involve trial and error. You are bound to have a recipe fail—that is just a part of the process . . . and a part of the fun!

With a solid basis of understanding how basic cookie baking science works, I hope this book will keep those mishaps to a minimum during your baking adventures.

Amanda

Let's Get Baking

No matter what we do, we cannot escape the fact that baking is a science. Therefore, we will need the right tools and ingredients to have success in baking the recipes in this book and developing our own flavor profiles. These are the absolute must-haves for the best outcome using this book and learning and growing as a baker.

TOOLS OF THE TRADE

A big part of good baking comes down to having the right tools on hand. The good news is, when it comes to cookies, there aren't too many tools you actually need, and you likely already have many of them.

DRY MEASURING CUPS & SPOONS

Every good baker should have a good set of dry measuring cups and spoons. This means a set that is simple in design and allows you to spoon and sweep your ingredients for accurate measuring. For more on measuring dry ingredients, see page 12.

LIQUID MEASURING CUPS & ADJUSTABLE MEASURING CUPS

You should also keep a set of liquid measuring cups, which are necessary for measuring such ingredients as oil, milk and water. A good set should come with containers that can measure at least a cup (240 ml) and as small as a couple of tablespoons (about 30 ml). If you are serious about accuracy (and, trust me, we are here), an adjustable measuring cup is perfect for measuring liquid, dry and especially sticky ingredients. You can find one inexpensively online. For more on measuring wet ingredients, see page 12.

KITCHEN SCALE

A lot of home bakers shy away from using a kitchen scale for weighing their ingredients when baking. It can feel too tedious or like an unnecessary item taking up space in your kitchen, but for the most accurate measurements and consistently good cookies, it is a must. In fact, there is a chapter where you will be required to use a kitchen scale. It, honestly, is a game changer and will make measuring ingredients faster and easier.

COOKIE SCOOPS

Using cookie scoops helps ensure that your cookies are all uniform in size. This is important for making sure each cookie is done baking at the same time and you aren't left with any that are drastically bigger or smaller than the rest. I prefer a scoop that is about 1½ to 2 tablespoons big. This roughly translates to 1½ to 1¾ inches (4 to 4.5 cm) in diameter, or 35 to 48 g.

BAKING SHEETS

Everyone has a preference for baking sheets. All the recipes in this book are baked on rimmed baking sheets. I recommend a heavy-duty, rimmed aluminum sheet, such as the ones from Nordic Ware™. You can use rimless cookie sheets, but understand that the cookies will brown faster and therefore require a shorter baking time.

OVEN THERMOMETER

Believe it or not, most ovens are not accurately calibrated or they heat unevenly. You might be able to get away with it when making a chocolate chip cookie, but if you want to make gorgeous meringues or macarons, you need to know exactly what is going on inside your oven. An oven thermometer will let you know whether your oven is correctly calibrated and whether it has any hot or cold spots.

STAND MIXER

I make almost all my cookies with a stand mixer because it makes the job faster and easier. You can use a handheld mixer, but it may prove too difficult to use for many of the denser doughs, so I always advise to opt for a stand mixer whenever possible.

SELECTING YOUR INGREDIENTS

The right ingredients can often make or break a recipe. I always recommend using the highest quality you can afford whenever possible. However, store-brand products can work just as well as the name-brand ingredients in most recipes if you cannot afford to splurge during your cookie baking experiments. I will say that when a particular ingredient is a big feature of a recipe, you may want to splurge regardless—for example, try using your favorite name-brand unsalted butter in your macaron frosting instead of the store-brand, because the flavor of the frosting is very prominent in a macaron.

I try to keep specialty ingredients to a minimum in this book, so you can find just about everything at your local grocery stores. If there is a specific ingredient or brand you need to use, that will be annotated within the recipe itself.

When you are first starting out with these recipes, I recommend sticking to the recipes as written before experimenting with substitutions. I will always give ideas for substitutions that I know will work for you when possible. Some substitutions won't make a huge difference (such as stick margarine versus stick unsalted butter in a soft chocolate chip cookie), whereas others will end in tears (such as replacing the almond flour with all-purpose flour in your macarons).

General rules of thumb: You can use either light or dark brown sugar in a recipe that calls simply for brown sugar. Both types contain molasses, but dark brown sugar contains more molasses. The reason that a recipe might specify one or the other will depend on how much molasses flavor should impact the final flavor profile. If a recipe contains only granulated sugar, it is called simply sugar. You can use natural unsweetened cocoa powder or Dutch-processed cocoa powder in any recipe that calls for cocoa powder, unless the type is specified.

Instead of going into the details about exactly what brands you should use or what percentage chocolate bar I recommend for a cookie, look out for my tips and suggestions as they come throughout the book.

MEASURING AND PREPPING YOUR INGREDIENTS

Before you begin mixing together ingredients, you need to be sure they are properly measured. It isn't as obvious as you may think.

Use a scale: For the best results, you should use a kitchen scale that provides precise metric weights. It makes your life easier at the end of the day, because weighing ingredients means you are getting a more accurate final product that will be exactly the same each time you make it. Let's review some key measuring tips if you are still hesitant to move to the weight measurements provided in the book. These tips are important because by weighing by volume, you are at the mercy of how carefully you have added your dry goods to your measuring cups. These tips should help you be a little more accurate.

Measuring flour, powdered sugar and other similar ingredients: You should first give your ingredient a light fluffing. I like to do this by taking a fork and swishing it around in the container. This is because ingredients such as flour tend to settle and compact over time. Once you've fluffed the ingredient, use a spoon to scoop the ingredient into the measuring cup until it fully fills the cup. Use the straight edge of an object, such as the back of a knife, to sweep off the excess so that the ingredient is level with the top of the cup.

Measuring light and brown sugar: Brown sugar should be measured in a dry measuring cup, lightly packed into the cup and then leveled off at the top. To lightly pack, fill your measuring cup with the brown sugar, gently pat it down, then brush off any excess. If a recipe calls for tightly packed brown sugar, press down as firmly as you can into the measuring cup and add as much as you can to create a level amount of sugar.

Measuring wet ingredients: Wet ingredients should be measured with liquid measuring cups. Leave the cup on a flat surface as you pour in the ingredient and get eye level with the measuring marks on the cup to read an accurate measurement. I like getting a nesting set of measuring cups, like the set from OXO™. I also recommend an adjustable liquid measuring cup if you want to cut back on items in your kitchen. It is also especially good for stickier ingredients, such as honey and molasses, as you simply push out the ingredient without needing to scrape out all the rest left behind in a conventional cup.

Measuring thicker "wet" ingredients: Such ingredients as peanut butter and applesauce are typically included on the wet ingredients side of the spectrum, but you should still use a dry measuring cup to accurately measure these ingredients. You can lightly grease the cup when measuring sticky ingredients, such as peanut butter.

Mise en place: This means "everything in its place." Read the recipe carefully—twice if you need to—and measure out all your ingredients before you begin. This is an important practice to use when baking (and cooking!), for many reasons. For one, it informs you right away whether you have all and enough of the ingredients you need for any given recipe. Also, some recipes depend on strict timing, and if you are pausing between steps to find and measure ingredients, you may end up accidentally ruining the final product.

To chill or not to chill: Some recipes ask you to chill the dough; others don't. A few recipes are specific in the amount of time you should chill the dough. There are two reasons for it. The first and most important is texture. Chilling the dough and allowing the butter to harden in the dough allows the flour to absorb the moisture we added to the dough. This will keep the dough from spreading too much. You don't have that issue with some cookie dough ratios, though, which is the beauty of those specific recipes. The other reason is flavor development. The longer you chill the dough, the more the flavors can meld together and create a more delicious cookie. The truth is, you can chill most cookie doughs, but the ones that don't have a chill time are the ones you want to come close to room temperature again before baking. Such cookies as meringues, fortune cookies and macarons are not made with a dough and are very temperamental and should never be chilled.

Freshman Cookies

The Best Drop Cookies

In this chapter, we are going to begin with the very basics. The classic cookies we all know and love, such as chocolate chip and sugar cookies, plus some surprise essential variations we need to know to be able to customize our cookies just how we want them. Don't be fooled, though: While these cookies are considered the starter level, the flavor development we create is anything but basic. We will learn how to change up how we prepare a simple ingredient, such as butter, to create a cookie that will instantly make you drool.

These cookies require less effort and technical know-how to make a big impact, which means that they are perfect for people just learning how to bake. An intermediate baker who wants to learn how to fine-tune their cookies to create the flavors and textures they want will also still benefit from the cookies in this section. Advanced bakers will love rediscovering old favorites, many with light twists and flavor combinations to spark their imagination, such as my favorite Malted Oatmeal Cookies (page 25) and Traditional *Pryaniki* (page 46).

Anything-but-Basic Chocolate Chip Cookies

Chocolate chip cookies are the most popular cookies in the world, and for good reason. Not only can you add things like nuts and dried fruits, but you can also play with the texture by changing ratios, ingredients and baking times. Here are three main ways to make the classic CCC.

Soft and Chewy

YIELDS 24 COOKIES

Here, we use cornstarch to help puff and lighten the texture of the cookie to aid in the softness. The higher brown sugar ratio, extra egg yolk and extra mixing time after adding the flour all contribute to the chewiness.

2½ cups (312 g) all-purpose flour

1 tsp baking soda

¾ tsp sea salt

1 tsp cornstarch

¾ cup (1½ sticks/170 g) unsalted butter, at room temperature

1 cup (220 g) firmly packed brown sugar

¾ cup (150 g) granulated sugar

1 large egg, at room temperature

1 large egg yolk, at room temperature

2½ tsp (12 ml) vanilla extract

1½ cups (255 g) chocolate chips

In a medium-sized bowl, whisk together the flour, baking soda, salt and cornstarch, then set aside.

In the bowl of a stand mixer fitted with the paddle attachment, beat together the butter, brown sugar and granulated sugar on medium speed until light and fluffy—this can take up to 3 to 5 minutes. Scrape the sides and bottom of the bowl. Beat in the egg, egg yolk and vanilla until well combined, another 2 to 3 minutes, then scrape the bowl again.

Gradually add the flour mixture to the butter mixture, mixing on low speed, until just incorporated. When there are no streaks of flour, mix for an additional minute. Fold in the chocolate chips, using a spatula, and mix just until they are evenly distributed.

Cover the cookie dough with plastic wrap and chill for at least an hour, preferably overnight for the best flavor development.

Line two rimmed baking sheets with parchment paper or silicone baking mats. Preheat the oven to 350°F (177°C). Portion the dough into balls that are roughly 1½ to 2 tablespoons (1½ to 1¾ inches [4 to 4.5 cm] or 35 to 45 g) big and place them about 2 inches (5 cm) apart on the prepared baking sheets.

Bake for 10 to 12 minutes, or until the edges of the cookies are a nice golden brown but the centers look slightly underdone. Remove the cookies from the oven and leave them on the baking sheets for about 1 minute to cool before transferring them to wire racks to cool completely.

You can store the cookies in an airtight container at room temperature for up to a week.

Thin and Crispy

YIELDS 24 COOKIES

For buttery thin and crispy cookies, we omit the cornstarch and lessen the baking soda. Using more granulated sugar removes the chewiness you get from using brown sugar, and the milk helps encourage the dough to spread. You will need to bake these in batches, so be prepared!

---

2 cups (250 g) all-purpose flour

½ tsp baking soda

¾ tsp sea salt

¾ cup (1½ sticks/170 g) unsalted butter, at room temperature

1 cup (200 g) granulated sugar

½ cup (110 g) brown sugar

1 large egg, at room temperature

3 tbsp (44 ml) milk, at room temperature

2½ tsp (12 ml) vanilla extract

1½ cups (255 g) chocolate chips

Preheat the oven to 375°F (191°C). Line two rimmed baking sheets with parchment paper or a silicone baking mat.

In a medium-sized bowl, whisk together the flour, baking soda and salt, then set aside.

In the bowl of a stand mixer fitted with the paddle attachment, beat together the butter, granulated sugar and brown sugar on medium speed until light and fluffy—this may take 4 to 5 minutes. Scrape the sides and bottom of the bowl with a spatula.

Add the egg, milk and vanilla to the butter mixture and beat for an additional 3 minutes. Scrape down the bowl again.

Add the flour mixture all at once and stir until just combined. Fold in the chocolate chips, using a spatula, and mix just until they are evenly distributed.

Portion out the dough into equal-sized balls 1½ to 2 tablespoons (1½ to 1¾ inches [4 to 4.5 cm] or 35 to 45 g) big. Equally space apart six balls on each of the two prepared baking sheets. Do not add more to each pan, as the cookies will spread quite a bit.

Bake for 13 to 15 minutes, or until the edges are a deep golden brown and the tops are a very light golden brown.

Remove the cookies from the oven and let them cool for 1 to 2 minutes on the baking sheets before transferring them to a wire rack to cool completely. Repeat with the remaining dough to bake another dozen cookies.

You can store the cookies in an airtight container at room temperature for up to a week.

Thick and Cakey

YIELDS 24 COOKIES

Thick, tender and cakey cookies use more cake flour, which has a lower protein content. Replacing the baking soda with baking powder also allows for more tenderness and rise. For even thicker cookies, replace half of the butter with butter-flavored shortening.

2½ cups (300 g) cake flour

1½ tsp (6 g) baking powder

¾ tsp salt

1 cup (2 sticks/227 g) unsalted butter, at room temperature

¾ cup (150 g) granulated sugar

1 cup (220 g) brown sugar

2 large eggs, at room temperature

2½ tsp (12 ml) vanilla extract

1½ cups (255 g) chocolate chips

Extra Credit: *There are so many ways to customize your CCCs. Adding dried fruits and/or nuts are the most popular, but you don't have to stop there. Experiment with spices, instant espresso or coffee, or adding chopped pieces of your favorite candies. Use them to sandwich ice cream, ganache or frosting. Replace graham crackers with these cookies to make the most decadent s'mores you've ever tasted. There is so much you can do with these cookies.*

In a medium-sized bowl, whisk together the cake flour, baking powder and salt, then set aside.

In the bowl of a stand mixer fitted with the paddle attachment, beat together the butter, granulated sugar and brown sugar on medium speed until light and fluffy—this can take up to 3 to 5 minutes. Scrape the sides and bottom of the bowl. Beat in the eggs and vanilla until well combined—another 2 to 3 minutes, then scrape the bowl again.

Gradually add the flour mixture to the butter mixture, mixing on low speed, until just incorporated and there are no streaks of flour.

Fold in the chocolate chips, using a spatula, and mix just until they are evenly distributed.

Cover the cookie dough with plastic wrap and chill for at least an hour, preferably overnight for the best flavor development.

Line three rimmed baking sheets with parchment paper or silicone baking mats. Preheat the oven to 350°F (177°C).

Portion the dough into balls that are roughly 1½ to 2 tablespoons (1½ to 1¾ inches [4 to 4.5 cm] or 35 to 45 g) big. Shape them more oval than round so they resemble eggs to help ensure you get a thicker cookie, and place them, on their shorter side, about 2 inches (5 cm) apart on the prepared baking sheets.

Bake for 10 to 12 minutes, or until the edges of the cookies are a nice golden brown but the centers look slightly underdone. Remove the cookies from the oven and leave them on the baking sheets for about 1 minute to cool before transferring them to wire racks to cool completely.

You can store the cookies in an airtight container at room temperature for up to a week.

Not-Your-Grandma's Oatmeal Cookies

Oatmeal cookies get a bad rap because of the oatmeal and the deceptive raisins that look suspiciously like chocolate. But oatmeal cookies are a great way to play with flavor and texture. These are so buttery and mouthwatering, they might just become your new favorite cookie. And yes, we are skipping the raisins and going straight to chocolate.

Chocolate Chunk Oatmeal Cookies

YIELDS 20 COOKIES

These are thick, chewy, soft and completely unlike any other oatmeal cookie you've tried. They have an incredible depth of flavor, thanks to the blend of sugars and chilling time, plus pools of melted chocolate in every bite. Everyone will actually want to grab two or three, or ten, of these!

1¾ cups (140 g) old-fashioned rolled oats

¾ cup (94 g) all-purpose flour

½ tsp baking soda

¾ tsp sea salt

⅔ cup (1⅓ sticks/151 g) unsalted butter, at room temperature

⅓ cup (73 g) packed light brown sugar

⅓ cup (67 g) granulated sugar

1 large egg, at room temperature

1 tsp vanilla extract

⅔ cup (113 g) chocolate chips

In a medium-sized bowl, whisk together the oats, flour, baking soda and salt, then set aside.

In the bowl of a stand mixer fitted with the paddle attachment, beat together the butter, brown sugar and granulated sugar on medium speed until light and fluffy—this should take 3 to 5 minutes. Scrape down the sides and bottom of your bowl.

Add the egg and vanilla, then beat for an additional 2 minutes. Scrape down the sides and bottom of the bowl again.

Gradually add the oat mixture to the butter mixture, mixing on low speed, until there are no streaks of flour. Fold in the chocolate chips, using a spatula, and mix just until they are evenly distributed. Cover the cookie dough with plastic wrap and chill for at least 2 hours, preferably overnight.

Preheat the oven to 350°F (177°C). Line two rimmed baking sheets with parchment paper or silicone baking mats.

Portion the dough into balls that are roughly 2 tablespoons (1¾ inches [4.5 cm] or 49 g) big and place them about 2 inches (5 cm) apart on the prepared baking sheets. Bake for 12 to 15 minutes, or until the cookies are a nice golden brown around the edges, but still look slightly underdone in the center.

Remove the cookies from the oven and allow them to cool on the baking sheets for about 2 minutes before carefully transferring them to a wire rack to cool completely.

Store the cookies in an airtight container at room temperature for up to 5 days.

Malted Oatmeal Cookies

YIELDS 24 COOKIES

Like the version we just made, these cookies are incredibly soft and chewy, but with a complex flavor you won't find at your local stores. The mix of espresso and malt give these cookies a nostalgic kick that will have you craving them all the time. Malted milk powder is used to make those old-fashioned malt drinks and is usually found in your grocery store near the powdered chocolate milk mixes.

1 cup (125 g) all-purpose flour

1⅔ cups (133 g) old-fashioned oats

¾ tsp sea salt

¾ tsp baking soda

¼ tsp baking powder

½ cup (1 stick/114 g) unsalted butter, at room temperature

½ cup (110 g) lightly packed light brown sugar

⅓ cup (67 g) granulated sugar

1 tbsp (16 g) espresso powder

⅓ cup (40 g) malted milk powder

1 large egg, at room temperature

2 tbsp (42 g) honey

2 tsp (10 ml) vanilla extract

⅓ cup (56 g) chopped chocolate

In a medium-sized bowl, whisk together the flour, oats, salt, baking soda and baking powder, then set aside.

In the bowl of a stand mixer fitted with the paddle attachment, beat together the butter, brown sugar and granulated sugar on medium speed until light and fluffy, about 5 minutes.

Mix the espresso powder and malted milk powder into the butter mixture until fully incorporated, about another 2 minutes, scraping down the sides and bottom of the bowl as needed.

Beat in the egg, honey and vanilla into the butter mixture. Mix for about another 2 minutes and again scrape the sides and bottom of the bowl.

Add the oat mixture and stir until just combined and there are no streaks of flour. Fold in the chocolate, using a spatula.

Cover the bowl with plastic wrap and chill for at least an hour, or overnight for full flavor development.

Preheat the oven to 350°F (177°C) and line two rimmed baking sheets with parchment paper or silicone baking mats.

Portion the dough into balls that are 2 tablespoons (1¾ inches [4.5 cm] or 49 g) big. Place them at least 2 inches (5 cm) apart on the prepared baking sheets.

Bake for 13 to 15 minutes, or until the cookie edges look set and they are a deep golden brown color. Remove from the oven, then leave on the baking sheet for about 2 minutes before transferring to a wire rack to cool completely.

You can store the cookies in an airtight container at room temperature for up to 5 days.

Your New Favorite Sugar Cookies

YIELDS 20 COOKIES

Sugar cookies sometimes get confused with snickerdoodles, but they actually lack the cream of tartar that gives snickerdoodles their classic puffiness and flavor. Instead, these are thick, soft and chewy cookies that seem to almost melt in your mouth. They are the perfect canvas to infuse with just about any flavor you can imagine. Unlike traditional sugar cookies, for this recipe, I like to add a touch of brown sugar to help boost the flavor. See the Extra Credit section for more ideas!

2½ cups (313 g) all-purpose flour

2 tsp (4 g) cornstarch

½ tsp baking powder

½ tsp sea salt

1 cup (200 g) granulated sugar, plus more for rolling

¼ cup (55 g) light brown sugar

1 cup (2 sticks/227 g) unsalted butter, at room temperature

1 tsp vanilla extract

1 large egg, at room temperature

Extra Credit: *You can infuse the cookies with citrus flavor by adding 2 teaspoons (4 g) of zest along with the sugar while creaming the butter and sugar together. You can also take a teaspoon of zest and rub it in the granulated sugar you roll the cookies in. For a pop of color and flavor, you can process an ounce (28 g) of freeze-dried fruit until it becomes a powder and add it to the granulated sugar you use to roll the cookies in.*

In a medium-sized bowl, whisk together the flour, cornstarch, baking powder and salt, then set aside.

In the bowl of a stand mixer fitted with the paddle attachment, beat together the granulated sugar, brown sugar and butter on medium speed until light and fluffy—this should take 3 to 4 minutes.

Scrape down the sides and bottom of your bowl, then add the vanilla and egg. Beat for about another minute, or until the mixture is fully incorporated, about another 2 minutes. Scrape down the sides and bottom of the bowl as needed.

Gradually add the flour mixture, mixing on low speed, until just combined and there are no streaks of flour.

Place some granulated sugar in a bowl. Portion the dough into balls that are about 2 tablespoons (1¾ inches [4.5 cm] or 45 g) big, and shape into a ball with the palms of your hands. Roll the dough balls in the sugar until fully coated.

Place the coated dough balls on parchment-lined rimmed baking sheets and chill for 15 to 20 minutes. While the dough is chilling, preheat the oven to 350°F (177°C).

Separate the dough balls so they are at least 2 inches (5 cm) apart, then bake for 10 to 12 minutes, or until the cookies have spread a bit, are puffy and are just beginning to show signs of light browning on the edges.

Remove from the oven. Allow the cookies to cool on the baking sheets for 1 minute before transferring to a wire rack to cool completely.

Store the cookies in an airtight container at room temperature for up to a week.

Pillowy Soft Peanut Butter Cookies

YIELDS 28 COOKIES

Behold! The absolute best peanut butter cookie you will ever meet. This is the type of cookie you end up accidentally eating an entire batch of in one day. They're deeply peanut buttery and sincerely delightful. These are very similar to sugar cookies; however, we need to adjust for the way peanut butter can weigh down a cookie dough and complement the flavor by favoring brown sugar over granulated.

---

1 cup (2 sticks/227 g) unsalted butter

2⅓ cups (292 g) all-purpose flour

1 tsp baking soda

¾ tsp sea salt

1½ cups (330 g) packed light brown sugar

2 large eggs, at room temperature

1 tbsp (15 ml) vanilla extract

1 cup (255 g) smooth peanut butter

1 cup (200 g) granulated sugar for rolling

In a small saucepan, melt your butter over low heat. Pour the melted butter into the bowl of your stand mixer and let cool to room temperature.

In a medium-sized bowl whisk together the flour, baking soda and salt, then set aside.

Fit the stand mixer with the paddle attachment, add the brown sugar to the cooled butter, then beat on medium speed until well combined, about 3 minutes.

Add the eggs and vanilla to the butter mixture, then mix for another 2 to 3 minutes. Mix in the peanut butter and beat for an additional 3 minutes. Scrape down the sides and bottom of the bowl as needed.

Gradually add the flour mixture to the butter mixture, mixing on low speed, until just incorporated and there are no streaks of flour.

Cover the cookie dough with plastic wrap and let chill for at least an hour.

Preheat the oven to 350°F (177°C) and line two rimmed baking sheets with parchment paper or silicone baking mats.

Pour the granulated sugar into a bowl. Portion the dough into balls about 2 tablespoons (1¾ inches [4.5 cm] or 45 g) big and roll into balls. Roll the balls in the granulated sugar until fully coated.

Place the coated dough balls about 2 inches (5 cm) apart on the prepared baking sheets and bake for about 14 minutes, or until the cookies are golden brown on the edges and are puffy.

Remove the cookies from the oven and allow them to rest on the baking sheets for 1 minute before transferring them to wire racks to cool completely.

Store the cookies in an airtight container at room temperature for up to a week.

Melt-in-Your-Mouth Sour Cream Cookies

YIELD 20 COOKIES

Sour cream gives these cookies a wonderful tanginess. It also makes them so soft and cakelike, thanks to how the acidity in the sour cream reacts to the baking soda and baking powder. They're like little pillows topped with a creamy frosting. To emphasize the creaminess and tanginess of the sour cream in the cookies, we use a sour cream frosting, which is great to decorate but also means we need to store any frosted cookies in the refrigerator.

1¾ cups (219 g) all-purpose flour

1 tsp baking powder

½ tsp baking soda

¼ tsp sea salt

½ cup (1 stick/114 g) unsalted butter, at room temperature

¾ cup (150 g) granulated sugar

½ cup (115 g) sour cream, at room temperature

1 large egg, at room temperature

1½ tsp (8 ml) vanilla extract

FROSTING

¼ cup (½ stick/57 g) unsalted butter, at room temperature

3 tbsp (45 g) sour cream, at room temperature

1½ cups (180 g) powdered sugar

1 tsp vanilla extract

⅛ tsp sea salt

Sprinkles, for decoration

In a small bowl, whisk together the flour, baking powder, baking soda and salt, then set aside.

In the bowl of a stand mixer fitted with the paddle attachment, beat together the butter and granulated sugar on medium speed until light and fluffy, about 4 minutes.

Add the sour cream and beat until well combined. Scrape down the sides and bottom of the bowl as needed. Add the egg and vanilla and beat until well incorporated.

Slowly stir in the flour mixture until just combined.

Cover the cookie dough with plastic wrap and chill for at least an hour. Preheat the oven to 350°F (177°C) and line two baking sheets with parchment paper or silicone baking mats. Remove the dough from the refrigerator.

Portion the dough into balls that are 1½ tablespoons (1½ inches [4 cm] or 35 g) big. Place them about 2 inches (5 cm) apart on the prepared baking sheets.

Bake for 10 minutes, or until the cookies are puffy and the edges are a light golden brown. Remove from the oven and allow the cookies to cool on the baking sheets for 2 minutes before transferring to a wire rack.

As the cookies cool, make the frosting: In the bowl of your stand mixer fitted with the paddle attachment, combine the butter and sour cream, and beat until smooth.

Add the powdered sugar and mix until combined. Add the vanilla and salt, and stir until well combined. Spread the frosting onto the cookies and top with sprinkles.

You can store the cookies in an airtight container in the refrigerator for up to 3 days.

Ultimate Brownie Cookies

YIELDS 22 COOKIES

These cookies are deeply chocolaty and fudgy. The recipe is adapted from a favorite brownie on my website to create a soft cookie that keeps true to all the best parts of both desserts in one. We do this by increasing the flour and decreasing the butter, to prevent them from spreading.

---

8 oz (225 g) semisweet chocolate, coarsely chopped

¾ cup (94 g) all-purpose flour

¼ cup (21 g) Dutch-processed cocoa powder

2 tsp (4 g) instant espresso powder

½ tsp baking powder

¼ tsp sea salt

6 tbsp (84 g) unsalted butter, at room temperature

¾ cup (165 g) packed dark brown sugar

¼ cup (50 g) granulated sugar

2 large eggs, at room temperature

1 tsp vanilla extract

¾ cup (135 g) chopped dark or milk chocolate (optional)

In a small, microwave-safe bowl, microwave the semisweet chocolate for 30 seconds. Remove from the microwave and stir well. If needed, microwave again for another 30 seconds. If, for any reason, the chocolate still has not completely melted after stirring, you may microwave it for an additional 15 seconds. Stir well until the chocolate is completely melted. Set aside to cool until needed.

In a small bowl, whisk together the flour, cocoa powder, espresso powder, baking powder and salt until well combined, then set aside.

In the bowl of a stand mixer fitted with the paddle attachment, beat together the butter, brown sugar and granulated sugar on medium speed until light and fluffy—this should take about 5 minutes.

Add the eggs and vanilla to the butter mixture and beat until fully incorporated, about another 3 minutes. Scrape down the sides and bottom of the bowl as needed.

Slowly drizzle the cooled chocolate into the butter mixture while the mixer is still running on low speed. Allow the mixer to beat in the chocolate for 2 to 3 minutes once it is completely poured in.

Fold in the flour mixture, and mix until just combined and there are no streaks of flour.

Fold in the chopped chocolate (if using).

Cover the cookie dough with plastic wrap and chill for only 30 minutes—any longer will prevent the cookies from being able to spread properly. Line two baking sheets with parchment paper or silicone baking mats.

Remove the dough from the refrigerator and preheat the oven to 350°F (177°C).

Portion the dough into balls that are about 1½ tablespoons (1½ inches [4 cm] or 35 g) big. Place them about 2 inches (5 cm) apart on the prepared baking sheets. Bake for 12 minutes, or until the dough is puffed on top and the edges are set.

Remove from the oven and allow to cool on the baking sheet for about 1 minute before transferring to a wire rack to cool completely.

Store the cookies in an airtight container at room temperature for up to a week.

Brown Butter Coconut Chocolate Chip Cookies

YIELDS 20 COOKIES

There is something about brown butter in cookies that really elevates everything. Brown butter is also known as beurre noisette, *which translates from French to "hazelnut butter," for its nutty aroma and flavor. It is a simple but incredible technique we will employ here and in future recipes. Coconut extract is optional, but really gives the unsweetened coconut a nice boost.*

1 cup (2 sticks/227 g) unsalted butter, cubed

1½ cups (120 g) shredded unsweetened coconut

¾ cup (150 g) granulated sugar

1 cup (220 g) packed brown sugar

2 large eggs, at room temperature

½ tsp coconut extract (optional)

2 tsp (10 ml) vanilla extract

2 cups (250 g) all-purpose flour

1½ tsp (6 g) baking powder

½ tsp sea salt

¾ cup (128 g) semisweet chocolate chips

In a medium-sized saucepan or skillet, heat the butter over medium heat while stirring frequently. Continue to cook until it begins to turn brown and smells nutty. Once the butter is a deep golden-brown or amber color, remove it from the heat. The butter can burn if you aren't careful, so pay attention once you notice the bubbling starting to slow down and clear up. Transfer to a heatproof container to cool completely, then refrigerate until it is almost but not completely solidified.

Place the shredded coconut in a clean, dry medium-sized skillet while the butter is chilling and stir frequently over medium heat until it smells fragrant and most of the coconut is a light golden-brown. Make sure you are using unsweetened coconut for the best coconut flavor! Remove from the heat.

In the bowl of a stand mixer fitted with the paddle attachment, immediately combine the toasted coconut with the brown butter, granulated sugar and brown sugar. Beat on medium speed until well mixed, about 5 minutes. This helps infuse the sugar and butter with the just-released coconut oils.

Beat in the eggs, coconut extract (if using) and vanilla. Mix for another 2 minutes. Scrape down the sides and bottom of the bowl as needed.

In a small bowl, whisk together the flour, baking powder and salt. Add the flour mixture to the butter mixture and stir until there are no streaks of flour. Fold in the chocolate chips.

Cover the dough with plastic wrap and chill for at least an hour, or overnight for the best flavor development.

Preheat the oven to 350°F (177°C) and line two baking sheets with parchment paper.

Portion the dough into balls that are about 2 tablespoons (1¾ inches [4.5 cm] or 45 g) big and place them about 2 inches (5 cm) apart on the prepared baking sheets. Bake for 10 to 12 minutes, or until the edges are a nice golden brown. Remove from the oven and allow to cool on the baking sheet for about 1 minute before transferring to a wire rack.

You can store the cookies in an airtight container at room temperature for up to a week.

Brown Butter Crinkle Cookies

YIELDS 22 COOKIES

Brown butter is such an amazing ingredient in cookies, it had to be the star of one! Crinkle cookies have a reputation for being a little tricky to make and get those deliciously famous crinkles. The trick is to chill the dough and roll the balls in both granulated and powdered sugar. You really want to pack on the powdered sugar and not be tempted to shake off any excess.

⅔ cup (1⅓ sticks/151 g) unsalted butter

2¼ cups (281 g) all-purpose flour

1 tbsp (5 g) Dutch-processed cocoa powder

¾ tsp baking powder

2 tsp (4 g) espresso powder

½ tsp ground cinnamon

½ tsp sea salt

⅔ cup (133 g) granulated sugar

½ cup (110 g) packed brown sugar

2 large eggs, at room temperature

1 tsp vanilla extract

COATING
½ cup (100 g) granulated sugar

1½ cups (180 g) powdered sugar

In a medium-sized saucepan or skillet, heat the butter over medium heat while stirring frequently. Continue to cook until it begins to turn brown and smells nutty. The butter can burn if you aren't careful, so pay close attention once you notice the bubbling start to slow down and clear up. Once the butter is a deep golden brown or amber color, remove from the heat and transfer to a heatproof container to cool completely. Chill in the refrigerator until it is almost but not completely solidified.

In a small bowl, whisk together the flour, cocoa powder, baking powder, espresso powder, cinnamon and salt, then set aside.

In the bowl of a stand mixer fitted with the paddle attachment, beat together the brown butter, granulated sugar and brown sugar on medium speed for about 5 minutes, or until light and fluffy.

Add the eggs and vanilla to the butter mixture. Beat until well combined, at least another 2 minutes. Scrape down the sides and bottom of the bowl as needed.

Stir in the flour mixture, and mix until just incorporated and there are no streaks of flour. Cover with plastic wrap and chill for at least an hour.

Preheat the oven to 350°F (177°C). Line two baking sheets with parchment paper. Place the granulated sugar for coating in one bowl, and the powdered sugar in another bowl.

Portion the dough into balls that are 1½ tablespoons (1½ inches [4 cm] or 35 g) big. Roll the balls lightly in the granulated sugar, then immediately place in the powdered sugar, fully coating and gently pressing the powdered sugar onto the dough. Do not shake off the excess powdered sugar.

Place the coated dough balls about 2 inches (5 cm) apart on the prepared baking sheets, then bake for about 15 minutes, or until the cookies are slightly puffed and cracked. The edges should look set, while the centers still look slightly underdone through the cracks.

Remove from the oven and allow to cool on the baking sheet for 1 minute before transferring to a wire rack to cool completely.

Store the cookies in an airtight container at room temperature for up to a week.

Apple Butter Snickerdoodles

YIELDS 20 COOKIES

These cookies are like a taste of autumn in every bite. They're full of apple and spice flavor, and adding brown butter and using brown sugar works to deepen the flavors. The secret is cooking down apple butter even further to concentrate the flavor even more.

1 cup + 2 tbsp (2 sticks + 2 tbsp/ 255 g) unsalted butter

½ cup (120 g) apple butter

2¼ cups (281 g) all-purpose flour

2 tsp (4 g) cream of tartar

1 tsp baking soda

1 tsp ground cinnamon

½ tsp ground ginger

½ tsp ground cardamom

¼ tsp ground nutmeg

¼ tsp ground allspice

½ tsp sea salt

1 cup (220 g) brown sugar

1 large egg, at room temperature

1 tsp vanilla extract

COATING
½ cup (100 g) granulated sugar

1 tsp ground cinnamon

In a small saucepan, heat the butter over medium heat, stirring it occasionally with a wooden spoon or whisk, until it turns brown and smells nutty. Watch carefully, as it can burn quickly if you aren't watching. Transfer to the bowl of your stand mixer and let cool to room temperature.

In a separate small saucepan, heat the apple butter over medium-low heat. Cook until the mixture thickens and is about ⅓ cup (80 g) in volume. Set aside to cool to room temperature.

In a medium-sized bowl, whisk together the flour, cream of tartar, baking soda, cinnamon, ginger, cardamom, nutmeg, allspice and salt, then set aside.

Fit the paddle attachment to your stand mixer and beat the butter and brown sugar together on medium speed until light and fluffy, 4 to 5 minutes. Scrape the sides and bottom of the bowl as needed.

Add the reduced apple butter, egg and vanilla, then beat for another minute on medium speed to fully combine.

Mix in the flour mixture on low speed until just incorporated.

Cover with plastic wrap and chill for at least an hour, preferably overnight.

Preheat the oven to 250°F (177°C) and line two baking sheets with parchment paper or silicone baking mats.

In a small bowl, stir together the granulated sugar and cinnamon. Portion the dough into balls that are about 2 tablespoons (1¾ inches [4.5 cm] or 45 g) big. Pour the cinnamon sugar into a small bowl. Roll the cookie dough balls in the cinnamon sugar.

Place the coated dough balls at least 2 inches (5 cm) apart on the prepared baking sheets.

Bake for 10 to 12 minutes, or until the edges are golden brown and the cookies are puffy.

Remove from the oven and let cool on the baking sheets for at least 2 minutes before transferring to a wire rack to cool completely.

Store in an airtight container for up to a week at room temperature.

Banana Bread Cookies

YIELDS 20 COOKIES

These are soft, moist cookies that taste just like banana bread. We cook down the banana to concentrate the banana flavor even more, then add walnuts and cream cheese frosting to make these cookies an unforgettable treat.

½ cup (112 g) mashed ripe banana

1⅔ cups (208 g) all-purpose flour

1 tsp cornstarch

1½ tsp (6 g) baking powder

½ tsp baking soda

½ tsp ground cinnamon

½ tsp sea salt

1 cup (220 g) brown sugar

5 tbsp (71 g) unsalted butter, at room temperature

1 tsp vanilla extract

1 large egg, at room temperature

½ cup (56 g) chopped walnuts (optional)

FROSTING

½ cup (115 g) cream cheese, at room temperature

3 tbsp (43 g) unsalted butter, at room temperature

¾ cup (90 g) powdered sugar

½ tsp vanilla extract

¼ tsp ground cinnamon

½ cup (56 g) chopped walnuts, for topping

In a small saucepan, heat the mashed banana over medium-low heat until it concentrates and cooks down to roughly 6 tablespoons (84 g). It will turn brown and smell very fragrant. You should be able to see the bottom of the pan when you use a wooden spoon to swipe the bottom of the pan. Remove from the heat and set aside to cool to room temperature. This can be done up to a day ahead, if you want.

In a small bowl, whisk together the flour, cornstarch, baking powder, baking soda, cinnamon and salt, then set aside.

In the bowl of a stand mixer fitted with the paddle attachment, beat together the cooled banana, brown sugar and butter on medium speed until light and fluffy, 4 to 5 minutes.

Add the vanilla and egg to the banana mixture, and beat on medium speed for another 2 to 3 minutes to fully combine. Scrape the sides and bottom of the bowl.

Mix in the flour mixture on low speed until just incorporated. Fold in the chopped walnuts (if using).

Cover the dough with plastic wrap and chill for at least 30 minutes. Preheat the oven to 350°F (177°C) and line two baking sheets with parchment paper or silicone baking mats.

Portion the dough into balls that are about 2 tablespoons (1¾ inches [4.5 cm] or 45 g) big. Place them at least 2 inches (5 cm) apart on the prepared baking sheets.

Bake for 10 to 12 minutes, or until the edges are golden brown. Remove from the oven and let cool on the baking sheets for 1 minute before transferring to a wire rack to cool completely.

While the cookies cool, make the frosting. In a small bowl, using a balloon whisk, beat together the cream cheese, butter, powdered sugar, vanilla and cinnamon until smooth. Top the cookies with the frosting, then top with more walnuts.

Store in an airtight container for up to a week at room temperature.

Blueberry Muffin Cookies

YIELDS 20 COOKIES

If you've ever wanted a cookie that was also half muffin and yet a thousand times better than both, this is for you. Buttery with a hint of lemon and pops of blueberry, all finished with a crunchy streusel topping—it's a cookie you'll be tempted to bake for breakfast. This also happens to be a great way to practice handling a less than neat dough, since the blueberries can get messy. I like using wild frozen blueberries. Or you can use ¾ cup (109 g) of fresh or (116 g) frozen regular blueberries.

STREUSEL

2 tbsp (28 g) unsalted butter, at room temperature

⅓ cup (42 g) all-purpose flour

3 tbsp (41 g) tightly packed brown sugar

½ tsp ground cinnamon

¼ tsp sea salt

COOKIE DOUGH

2½ cups (313 g) all-purpose flour

2 tsp (4 g) cornstarch

½ tsp baking powder

½ tsp sea salt

½ cup (100 g) granulated sugar, plus more for rolling

¾ cup (165 g) light brown sugar

1 cup (2 sticks/227 g) unsalted butter, at room temperature

1 tsp lemon zest

1 tsp vanilla extract

1 large egg, at room temperature

½ cup (80 g) wild blueberries

GLAZE (OPTIONAL)

1½ cups (180 g) powdered sugar

2 tbsp (30 ml) fresh lemon juice

1 tbsp (15 ml) heavy cream or milk

Make the streusel: In a small bowl, mix together the butter, flour, brown sugar, cinnamon and salt until they form crumbs. You can use a fork or clean hands to do this. Chill for 5 minutes.

Make the cookie dough: In a separate small bowl, whisk together the flour, cornstarch, baking powder and salt, then set aside.

In the bowl of a stand mixer fitted with the paddle attachment, beat together the granulated sugar, brown sugar, butter and zest on medium speed for 3 to 4 minutes, or until light and fluffy.

Add the vanilla and egg to the butter mixture, then beat for another 1 to 2 minutes, or until well combined.

Stir in the flour mixture until just combined. Use a rubber spatula to fold in the blueberries.

Portion the dough into balls that are 2 tablespoons (1¾ inches [4.5 cm] or 45 g) big. Dip one side of each dough ball in the streusel and gently pat to adhere.

Place on a rimmed baking sheet. Cover the dough with plastic wrap and chill for at least 30 minutes.

Preheat the oven to 350°F (177°C) and line two baking sheets with parchment paper or silicone baking mats.

Place the dough balls at least 2 inches (5 cm) apart on the prepared baking sheets.

Bake for 15 to 18 minutes, or until the edges look set and the streusel is a golden brown.

Remove from the oven and allow to cool on the baking sheets for 4 minutes before transferring to a wire rack to cool completely.

Make the glaze (if using): In a small bowl, using a whisk or fork, mix together the powdered sugar, lemon juice and cream or milk until smooth. Drizzle over the cooled cookies.

Store in an airtight container for up to 3 days in the refrigerator.

Coffee Cake Cookies

YIELDS 20 COOKIES

Being able to have your coffee cake in cookie form is a treat everyone needs to try at least once in their life. It is buttery and cinnamony, and the buttery streusel is otherworldly good. It is also good for practicing simple pairings (cookie and toppings) to make a deliciously complex cookie without needing to stuff or sandwich.

COOKIE DOUGH

1 cup + 2 tbsp (2 sticks + 2 tbsp/ 255 g) unsalted butter

2½ cups (313 g) all-purpose flour

1 tsp ground cinnamon

½ tsp sea salt

1 tsp baking soda

1½ cups (330 g) packed brown sugar

1 large egg, at room temperature

1 large egg yolk, at room temperature

1 tsp vanilla extract

STREUSEL

2 tbsp (28 g) unsalted butter, at room temperature

⅓ cup (42 g) all-purpose flour

3 tbsp (41 g) tightly packed brown sugar

½ tsp ground cinnamon

¼ tsp sea salt

GLAZE

1½ cups (180 g) powdered sugar

2 tbsp (30 ml) milk or cream

½ tsp vanilla extract

Make the cookie dough: In a small saucepan, heat the butter over medium heat, stirring occasionally with a wooden spoon or whisk, until it is golden brown and smells nutty. Be careful to watch the butter, as it can burn if you aren't paying attention. Transfer the butter to the bowl of your stand mixer and let cool to room temperature.

In a small bowl, whisk together the flour, cinnamon, salt and baking soda, then set aside.

Fit the paddle attachment to the mixer, add the brown sugar to the butter and beat on medium speed until light and fluffy, 3 to 4 minutes.

Add the egg, egg yolk and vanilla to the butter mixture, and beat on medium speed until fully combined, another 2 to 3 minutes. Scrape down the sides and bottom of the bowl as needed.

Mix in the flour mixture on low speed until just combined. Cover the dough with plastic wrap and chill for at least an hour.

Make the streusel: In a small bowl, mix together the butter, flour, sugar, cinnamon and salt until they form crumbs. You can use a fork or clean hands to do this. Chill for at least 5 minutes.

Preheat the oven to 350°F (177°C). Line two rimmed baking sheets with parchment paper or silicone baking mats.

Portion the dough into cookie dough balls that are about 2 tablespoons (1¾ inches [4.5 cm] or 45 g) big. Dip one side of each dough ball into the streusel and place them at least 2 inches (5 cm) apart on the prepared baking sheets.

Bake for 12 to 14 minutes, or until the edges and the streusel topping are both golden brown.

Remove from the oven and let cool on the baking sheet for 3 minutes before transferring to a wire rack to cool completely.

Store in an airtight container for up to a week at room temperature.

Traditional Pryaniki

YIELDS 50 COOKIES

I love these cookies because of the coffee and honey combined with the warm spices. This recipe also uses a new technique to make cookies. The dough needs rest time, but at room temperature— baking this dough while it is cold will result in a flatter cookie instead of the puffy cookie we want! It is a great reminder that there are so many ways to make a delicious drop cookie.

¼ cup (40 g) instant coffee granules

¼ cup (60 ml) hot water

½ cup (1 stick/114 g) unsalted butter

½ cup (100 g) granulated sugar

¾ cup (252 g) honey

1 large egg, at room temperature

¾ tsp baking soda

½ tsp white vinegar

¾ tsp baking powder

1 tsp vanilla extract

½ tsp ground allspice

½ tsp ground nutmeg

½ tsp ground ginger

¼ tsp freshly ground black pepper

½ tsp sea salt

1½ tsp (3 g) ground cardamom

1½ tsp (4 g) ground cinnamon

3½ cups (437 g) all-purpose flour

2½ cups (300 g) powdered sugar, for glaze

¼ cup (60 ml) milk, for glaze

In a medium-sized saucepan, combine the instant coffee and water and heat over low heat, stirring with a wooden spoon until the coffee dissolves.

Add the butter, granulated sugar and honey to the saucepan and increase the heat to medium. Bring the mixture to a boil for at least a minute, and stir with a whisk until the butter is melted, the sugar is dissolved and the mixture is well combined. Remove from the heat and transfer the mixture to a large bowl. Allow it to cool for at least 15 minutes.

Once cool, mix well with your wooden spoon as you add the egg, baking soda, vinegar and baking powder. Add the vanilla, allspice, nutmeg, ginger, pepper, salt, cardamom and cinnamon, then mix well again. Beat in the flour with your wooden spoon, mixing it in well until there are no streaks of flour.

Cover the bowl with plastic wrap and leave at room temperature for 4 hours, or chill it overnight. The dough bakes better when closer to room temperature, so if you have placed it in the refrigerator, leave the dough out at room temperature for at least 30 minutes before baking.

Preheat the oven to 325°F (163°C) and line three or four rimmed baking sheets with parchment paper or silicone baking mats.

Portion balls of dough that are 1 tablespoon (1¼ inches [3 cm] or 30 g) big and place them at least 1 inch (2.5 cm) apart on the prepared baking sheets. Bake for 20 to 25 minutes, or until they are puffed and the edges look set. Remove from the oven and leave on the baking sheets for 1 minute, then transfer to a wire rack to cool completely.

In a small bowl, stir together the powdered sugar and milk to make a glaze. Place paper towels under your wire rack and then dunk the cookies into the glaze so the top and bottom of each cookie is coated in the glaze. Let the excess drip off before transferring to the rack for the glaze to harden. Store in an airtight container for up to 2 weeks.

Extra Credit: *If you don't want to use coffee, you can replace the instant coffee granules with unsweetened cocoa powder. You can also flavor the glaze with a teaspoon of vanilla extract or lemon juice.*

Sophomore Cookies
Rolled and Shaped

I love cookies that require a little more time to put together. They allow for more flavor development and experimentation. But, they also require a little more patience and attention to the ingredients. Some may even need a little extra practice for the beginner baker to get just right, but they are still easy enough to master in time for the cookie exchange.

We are going to take what we learned from the previous level—how to make small adjustments to get the exact kind of cookie we want, such techniques as browning butter and enhancing flavors—and build upon them.

This chapter is all about learning how to work and manipulate cookie dough. We'll start off simple with classic thumbprint cookies (page 51), then understand how to get the perfect cutout cookies that don't spread, all while still learning more about using ingredients to create different flavor profiles. My favorite part? Learning why baking cookies two different ways is sometimes the best thing you could ever do to cookie dough.

Chocolate Pecan Pie Thumbprints

YIELDS 22 COOKIES

These tiny cookies are packed with so much flavor. Deep chocolate is paired with a pecan pie filling. I recommend using a darker Dutch-processed cocoa powder to balance the sweetness of the maple pecan filling.

COOKIE DOUGH

2⅓ cups (292 g) all-purpose flour

⅓ cup (28 g) Dutch-processed cocoa powder

½ tsp sea salt

1 cup (2 sticks/227 g) unsalted butter, at room temperature

⅔ cup (133 g) granulated sugar

1 large egg, at room temperature

1 tsp vanilla extract

Make the cookie dough: In a medium-sized bowl, whisk together the flour, cocoa powder and salt, then set aside.

In the bowl of a stand mixer fitted with the paddle attachment, beat together the butter and sugar on medium speed until light and fluffy—this should take 4 to 5 minutes.

Scrape down the sides and bottom of the bowl using a spatula, then add the egg and vanilla. Beat for 2 to 3 minutes, or until the mixture is fully combined and slightly paler in color.

Stir in the flour mixture, and mix until just incorporated and there are no streaks of flour.

Transfer the dough to another bowl, then cover with plastic wrap. Chill the dough while you make the filling, but no longer than 20 minutes, otherwise it can make the dough too difficult to handle.

Preheat the oven to 350°F (177°C). Line two baking sheets with parchment paper or silicone baking mats.

(continued)

Chocolate Pecan Pie Thumbprints
(Continued)

FILLING

3 tbsp (43 g) unsalted butter

3 tbsp (60 g) pure maple syrup

2 tbsp (26 g) brown sugar

1 large egg, at room temperature

½ tsp vanilla extract

¼ tsp sea salt

¾ cup (83 g) chopped unsalted pecans, plus some larger pieces for garnish

Make the filling: In a small saucepan, cook the butter over medium heat until it smells nutty and is brown in color—this can take about 10 minutes. The butter can burn if you aren't careful, so keep a close eye on it once the bubbles begin to slow down and clear up. Remove the butter from the heat and set aside to cool.

Add the maple syrup, brown sugar, egg, vanilla and salt to the browned butter, and whisk with a balloon whisk until just combined. Do not overmix or incorporate too much air into the mixture. Stir in the chopped pecans.

Roll the dough into balls that are about 1½ tablespoons (1½ inches [4 cm] or 35 g) big. Use your thumb or the end of a rounded wooden spoon to create an indentation in the top of each ball, taking care not to go through the ball. Use your fingers to press together any edges that may crack.

Place the dough balls, indented side up, 2 inches (5 cm) apart on the pre-pared baking sheets and fill the indentations with the pecan pie filling. The filling should be about level to the top of the cookie or slightly rounded, but not overflowing. Garnish with larger pieces of pecans.

Bake for 10 to 12 minutes, or until the edges of the cookies and the filling appears just set.

Remove the cookies from the oven and let them cool on the baking sheets for about 2 minutes before transferring them to a wire rack to cool completely.

You can store the cookies in an airtight container at room temperature for up to a week.

Blueberry Cheesecake Thumbprints

YIELDS 30 COOKIES

These are like little bite-sized cheesecakes, only better with the buttery cookie base. The sprinkling of freeze-dried blueberries is optional but helps accentuate the flavor of the blueberry jam. This is a great recipe to use with any flavor of cheesecake by swapping out the fruits or using caramel sauce instead.

COOKIE DOUGH

2¾ cups (344 g) all-purpose flour

1 tsp baking powder

½ tsp sea salt

1 cup (2 sticks/227 g) unsalted butter, at room temperature

1 cup (200 g) granulated sugar

1 large egg, at room temperature

2 tsp (10 ml) vanilla extract

½ cup (71 g) crushed graham crackers

Preheat the oven to 350°F (177°C) and line two baking sheets with parchment paper or silicone baking mats.

Make the cookie dough: In a medium-sized bowl, whisk together the flour, baking powder and salt, then set aside.

In the bowl of a stand mixer fitted with the paddle attachment, beat together the butter and granulated sugar on medium speed until light and fluffy, 4 to 5 minutes.

Scrape down the sides and bottom of the bowl with a spatula, then add the egg and vanilla. Beat for another 2 to 3 minutes, or until they are well combined. Scrape the bowl again.

Add the flour mixture and beat on low speed until just incorporated. Do not overmix. Place the graham cracker crumbs in a bowl.

Roll the dough into balls that are about 1½ tablespoons (1½ inches [4 cm] or 35 g) big, then roll them in the graham cracker crumbs.

Use the bottom of a rounded wooden spoon or your thumb to create an indentation in the top of each cookie ball; take care to not break through to the bottom of the ball. Use your hands to fix any cracks in the dough.

Place the dough balls, indented side up, about 2 inches (5 cm) apart on the prepared baking sheets.

Bake for 10 to 12 minutes, or until the edges are a light golden brown. Remove from the oven and allow them to cool on the baking sheet for a minute before transferring to a wire rack to cool. If the cookies have puffed, gently press down on the indentation again to create a well.

(continued)

Blueberry Cheesecake Thumbprints
(Continued)

FILLING

1 cup (160 g) fresh blueberries

¼ cup (50 g) granulated sugar

2 tsp (4 g) lemon zest

¼ tsp sea salt, divided

¼ cup (½ stick/57 g) unsalted butter, at room temperature

½ cup (115 g) cream cheese, at room temperature

1½ cups (180 g) powdered sugar

1 tsp vanilla extract

⅓ cup (13 g) freeze-dried blueberries, crushed, for topping (optional)

Make the filling: In a small saucepan, combine the blueberries, granulated sugar, zest and half of the salt, and cook over medium heat until the blueberries burst and the juices begin to thicken, 7 to 10 minutes. Remove from the heat and set aside to cool.

In a small bowl, using a balloon whisk, beat together the butter, cream cheese, powdered sugar, remaining salt and vanilla until fully mixed.

Dollop the cream cheese mixture into the cookie indentations so it almost reaches the top, then top with some of the homemade blueberry jam.

Finish by sprinkling the cookies with crushed freeze-dried blueberries, if desired.

Store the cookies in an airtight container at room temperature for up to a week.

Extra Credit: *This is a traditional thumbprint cookie base. You can fill it with a heaping teaspoon of your favorite jam (or enough that it reaches the top of the well without flowing over) and bake as normal for a typical thumbprint cookie. Replace a few tablespoons (about 30 g) of the flour with cocoa powder, then add red food coloring for a red velvet thumbprint cookie.*

Peanut Butter and Jelly Thumbprints

YIELDS 32 COOKIES

Who can resist PB&J? It is a favorite in my home. The crushed honey roasted peanuts in which we roll the cookie dough add a delightful texture and depth of flavor. Add a sprinkling of roughly chopped honey roasted peanuts to the top of the finished cookies for even more crunch.

1½ cups (187 g) all-purpose flour

1 tsp baking powder

¼ tsp sea salt

½ cup (1 stick/114 g) unsalted butter, at room temperature

⅔ cup (146 g) light brown sugar

½ cup (135 g) creamy peanut butter

1 large egg, at room temperature

1 tsp vanilla extract

⅓ cup (50 g) finely crushed honey roasted peanuts, for rolling

⅓ cup (67 g) granulated sugar, for rolling

1 cup (320 g) jam of your choice

Line two baking sheets with silicone baking mats. Preheat the oven to 350°F (177°C).

In a medium-sized bowl, whisk together the flour, baking powder and salt, then set aside.

In the bowl of a stand mixer fitted with the paddle attachment, beat the butter on medium speed until light, smooth and creamy—this should take 2 to 3 minutes. Add the brown sugar to the butter and beat on medium-high speed until the mixture is lighter in color and fluffy, about 5 minutes.

Add the peanut butter, egg and vanilla to the butter mixture, and beat on medium speed until well combined and of a light consistency—this should take another 2 to 4 minutes.

Add the flour mixture and mix on low speed until just combined. This should take just about a minute. Scrape the sides and bottom of the mixing bowl with a spatula after a few seconds to ensure everything is well incorporated.

In a small plate or bowl, stir together the peanuts and the granulated sugar.

Portion the dough into balls that are roughly 1 tablespoon (1¼ inches [3 cm] or 30 g) big. A cookie scoop works well here. Roll each ball into the peanut mixture.

Place the rolled balls roughly 1½ inches (4 cm) apart on the prepared baking sheets. Use the back of a rounded-end spatula or wooden spoon to create a deep indentation in the top of each ball of dough. The indentations should not reach or create a hole in the bottom of the dough. If the dough cracks, you can gently use your fingers to fix the cracks.

Bake the indented dough balls for 8 to 10 minutes, or until the cookies are a light golden brown at the bottom edges, then remove from the oven.

Do not let the cookies cool yet. Carefully fill the indentations with approximately 1 teaspoon of jam so that it reaches the top of the indentation but does not overflow. Place the cookies back in the oven and bake for another 4 to 5 minutes. The cookies will look slightly darker in color.

Remove from the oven and allow to cool on the baking sheets for about 1 minute before transferring to a wire rack to cool completely.

Store the cookies in an airtight container at room temperature for up to a week.

Buttery Shortbread

YIELDS APPROXIMATELY 20 COOKIES

Shortbread is so rich and buttery. In fact, it is defined by its high fat content and crumbly texture, compared to other cookies. It differs from a butter cookie, though, due to its lower sugar content. It makes a great base for certain tarts and bars, so it is a recipe that should be practiced. I love it paired with citrus to balance out the richness, but it's just as good when you lean into it and add chocolate and nuts. You can roll these out into shapes or flatten in a baking pan and simply score them.

½ cup (60 g) powdered sugar

½ tsp sea salt

1 cup (2 sticks/227 g) unsalted butter, cubed

1 tsp vanilla extract

2 cups (250 g) all-purpose flour, plus more for dusting

In a food processor, combine the sugar, salt and butter, and pulse until well mixed. Add the vanilla and pulse once or twice to incorporate it. Scrape the sides and bottom as needed.

Add the flour and pulse until just combined. Turn out the dough onto a sheet of plastic wrap and form into a large disk. Wrap tightly, then chill for 30 minutes.

Line a rimmed baking sheet with parchment paper or a silicone baking mat. Preheat the oven to 325°F (163°C).

Remove the dough from the refrigerator and unwrap. Place on a lightly floured surface and roll out until it is just over ¼ inch (6 mm) thick. If the dough cracks, you can take a piece from the edge and press it down around the crack to patch it up. You don't want cracks in your dough when you are cutting out shapes, as those cracks will show up in your final cookie. Cut out your shapes using a flour-dusted cookie cutter.

Place the cutouts 1 inch (2.5 cm) apart on the prepared baking sheet and bake for roughly 20 minutes for 3-inch (8-cm) cookies, or until the edges are a light golden brown. The time may vary greatly if you make larger or smaller cookies. If you bake them pressed into a pan and scored instead of cut with cookie cutters, you may want to add an additional 5 to 10 minutes.

Store in an airtight container for 2 weeks at room temperature.

Extra Credit: *You can do so much to infuse this shortbread with flavor. Add 1 to 2 teaspoons (2 to 4 g) of spices or herbs. You can also use 1 to 2 teaspoons (2 to 4 g) of any kind of citrus zest. Finely chopped nuts or chopped dried fruit (you want about ⅓ to ½ cup [50 to 75 g]) also makes a delicious addition.*

Chocolate Shortbread

YIELDS 16 COOKIES

Like the buttery shortbread, chocolate shortbread is a great base for tarts and dessert bars. It is also wonderful on its own or dipped in more chocolate. Because we don't use leavening in this recipe, you can use natural or Dutch-processed cocoa powder.

1 cup (125 g) all-purpose flour, plus more for dusting

½ cup (60 g) powdered sugar

¼ cup (21 g) unsweetened cocoa powder

¼ tsp sea salt

½ cup (1 stick/114 g) cold unsalted butter, cubed

½ tsp vanilla extract

In a food processor, combine the flour, sugar, cocoa powder and salt, and pulse to mix.

Add the butter and vanilla. Pulse again until the dough starts to come together.

Wrap the dough in plastic wrap and chill for about 30 minutes.

Place the dough on a lightly floured surface and sprinkle with a little more flour, then top with a sheet of parchment paper for easier rolling.

Roll out the dough until it is ¼ inch (6 mm) thick. Remove the top sheet of parchment paper. Cut out shapes that are about 3 inches (8 cm) across and place the cutouts 1 inch (2.5 cm) apart on a parchment-lined baking sheet.

Chill the cutouts on their pan while the oven preheats. Preheat the oven to 300°F (149°C).

Bake for 20 to 25 minutes, or until the edges are firm to the touch.

Remove from the oven and let cool on the baking sheet for about 1 minute before transferring to a wire rack to cool completely.

Store in an airtight container for up to 2 weeks at room temperature.

Banana Shortbread

YIELDS 18 COOKIES

Years ago, I tried this banana shortbread and it immediately became a favorite of mine. I think it's especially good if you pair it with salted caramel. For this recipe, we will be cutting the cookie into rounds, so we will be forming it first into a log to make easy work of that. This cookie also gets flipped and baked on both sides. We do this because shortbread is typically a drier cookie, so we need to give it help by battling the moisture in the banana without the cookie getting too brown on either side. It is still softer than your typical shortbread, but it only makes it that much more fun.

2½ cups (313 g) all-purpose flour

½ cup (48 g) almond flour

½ tsp sea salt

¼ tsp ground cinnamon

1 cup (2 sticks/227 g) unsalted butter, at room temperature

⅓ cup (76 g) mashed ripe banana

¾ cup (150 g) granulated sugar

1 tsp vanilla extract

In a medium-sized bowl, whisk together the all-purpose flour, almond flour, salt and cinnamon, then set aside.

In the bowl of a stand mixer fitted with the paddle attachment, beat together the butter, banana and sugar on medium speed until light and fluffy, 4 to 5 minutes.

Scrape the bottom and sides of the bowl, then add the vanilla and beat until combined, about another minute.

Add the flour mixture, and mix until just incorporated and there are no streaks of flour.

Place the dough on a sheet of plastic wrap and shape into a 2½-inch (7-cm)-wide, 14-inch (36-cm)-long log. You may need to chill the dough for about 20 minutes if the dough feels too soft to form into a log. Once it is formed into a log, wrap the dough in the plastic wrap and freeze for at least an hour or up to 4 hours.

Preheat the oven to 350°F (177°C) and line two baking sheets with parchment paper or silicone baking mats.

Remove the log from the freezer and unwrap it. Use a sharp knife to slice the log crosswise to create dough disks that are about ¼ inch (6 mm) thick, turning your log after each cut to keep the disks round. Place them at least 1 inch (2.5 cm) apart on the prepared baking sheets.

Bake for 10 to 11 minutes, or until the cookies are just starting to turn golden brown on the edges. Remove from the oven, flip the cookies over, then bake for another 1 to 2 minutes, or just until the golden edges become slightly more noticeable.

Remove from the oven and allow the cookies to cool on the baking sheets for about 2 minutes before transferring them to a wire rack.

Store in an airtight container for up to a week at room temperature.

Better-Than-Store-Bought Vanilla Wafers

YIELDS 30 COOKIES

As a kid, I used to love snacking on vanilla wafers. I am also a huge fan of banana pudding, of which vanilla wafers are a key ingredient. While the wafer ingredients are similar to that of shortbread and a roll-out sugar cookie, this recipe differs in the ratios and the use of powdered sugar, all of which leaves us with a flavorful, buttery and crisp cookie that is perfect for soaking up your pudding and bananas!

2 cups (250 g) all-purpose flour

¼ tsp sea salt

¾ cup + 2 tbsp (1½ sticks + 2 tbsp [199 g]) unsalted butter, at room temperature

1 cup (120 g) powdered sugar

1 large egg yolk, at room temperature

1 tsp vanilla extract

In a medium-sized bowl, whisk together the flour and salt, then set aside.

In the bowl of a stand mixer fitted with the paddle attachment, beat together the butter and sugar on medium speed for about 4 minutes, or until light and fluffy. Scrape down the sides and bottom of the bowl.

Add the egg yolk and vanilla to the butter mixture, and beat on medium speed for another minute. Scrape down the sides and bottom, if needed.

Stir in the flour mixture until just combined.

Place the dough on a sheet of plastic wrap. Roll it into two logs that are each about 10 inches (25 cm) long and just under 2 inches (5 cm) in diameter. You may need to chill the dough for about 20 minutes to make it easier to shape. Wrap each log in plastic wrap and chill for at least an hour.

Preheat the oven to 350°F (177°C) and line two rimmed baking sheets with parchment paper or a silicone baking mat.

Unwrap the dough and slice crosswise along each log to make disks that are about ¼ inch (6 mm) in diameter, turning the log slightly after every slice to keep each disk round. If the dough gets too soft, place in the freezer for about 5 minutes, or until firm again.

Place the disks about 1 inch (2.5 cm) apart on the prepared baking sheets.

Bake for 10 to 12 minutes, or until the edges are a nice golden brown. Remove from the oven and leave them on the baking sheets for 1 minute before transferring to a wire rack to cool completely.

Store the cookies in an airtight container for up to 2 weeks.

Chocolate and Vanilla Amaretti

YIELDS 14 COOKIES

Amaretti cookies are Italian almond cookies that have a slight resemblance to macarons (see page 144) in their ingredients, but they are instead worked into a dough to create an interior that is almost like marzipan. It is a great way to introduce you to beating egg whites and making sure you keep a clean bowl and whisk so they can reach soft peaks. It also teaches you about being careful and preparing yourself for handling a sticky dough. Hint: You'll want to dust your hands with powdered sugar often.

2 large egg whites, at room temperature

⅛ tsp sea salt

½ tsp almond extract

½ tsp vanilla extract

⅔ cup (133 g) granulated sugar

2 cups (200 g) almond flour

1½ tbsp (8 g) unsweetened cocoa powder

1 cup (120 g) powdered sugar, for coating

Extra Credit: *You can omit the chocolate and have just vanilla, or double the chocolate and add it to the entire dough. You can also add a teaspoon of lemon zest, or a teaspoon of ground cinnamon or any other spices. This also makes a great cookie to stuff. You can add chocolate chips or fill each ball with a surprise filling, such as soft caramel, ½ teaspoon of chocolate hazelnut spread or a nut butter.*

Preheat the oven to 325°F (160°C). Line a rimmed baking sheet with parchment paper or a silicone baking mat.

Thoroughly clean and dry your stand mixer bowl and whisk attachment. Combine the egg whites and salt in the bowl and beat on medium speed until soft peaks form. Soft peaks are when the egg whites have doubled or more in size, and when you lift your whisk out of the bowl and turn it upside down, you will see a soft fall or droop at the end—this can take between 4 and 6 minutes.

Add the almond and vanilla extracts and beat in well for about a minute.

Stir in the granulated sugar and flour, then mix until everything comes together like a sticky dough. This is not like making macarons, so no need to worry about overmixing or being delicate.

Divide the dough into two portions, placing one of them in a separate bowl, and add the cocoa powder to one of the portions. You can incorporate it by hand, or using your favorite mixing tool. It can be a sticky process.

Place your powdered sugar in a separate bowl. Take 1½ teaspoons (¾ inches in diameter or 12 g) of the regular dough and 1½ teaspoons (¾ inch in diameter or 12 g) of the chocolate dough and roll them together in your hands to form a ball. You can lightly dust your hands with powdered sugar to keep them from getting too sticky.

Roll the formed balls in the powdered sugar and ensure they are well coated.

Place the coated dough balls about an inch (2.5 cm) apart on your prepared baking sheet. Gently press the top of each to slightly flatten them just a little.

Bake for 23 to 25 minutes, or until cracks begin to form and the bottoms are just barely beginning to turn golden brown. Remove from the oven and allow to cool on the baking sheets for a minute before transferring to a wire rack to cool completely.

Store in an airtight container for up to a week.

Red Velvet Amaretti

YIELDS 14 COOKIES

I love the combination of amaretti and red velvet together. Seeing the red cracks in the cookies reminds me of the holidays. They're a simple yet delicious way to change up the cookie into something really special.

2 large egg whites, at room temperature

⅛ tsp sea salt

½ tsp almond extract

½ tsp vanilla extract

½ tsp gel red food coloring

⅔ cup (133 g) granulated sugar

2 cups (200 g) almond flour

1½ tbsp (8 g) unsweetened cocoa powder

1 cup (120 g) powdered sugar, for coating

Preheat the oven to 325°F (160°C). Line a rimmed baking sheet with parchment paper or a silicone baking mat.

Thoroughly clean and dry your stand mixer bowl and its whisk attachment. Combine the egg whites and salt in the bowl and beat on medium speed until soft peaks form. Soft peaks are when the egg whites have doubled or more in size, and when you lift your whisk out of the bowl and turn it upside down, you will see a soft fall or droop at the end—this can take between 4 and 6 minutes.

Add the almond and vanilla extracts, plus the food coloring, then beat on medium speed for about a minute.

Stir in the granulated sugar and almond flour, and mix until everything comes together like a sticky dough. This is not like making macarons, so no need to worry about overmixing or being delicate.

Place your powdered sugar in a bowl. Take a tablespoon (1¼ inches [3 cm] or 25 g) of the dough and roll to form a ball. You can lightly dust your hands with powdered sugar to keep them from getting too sticky.

Roll the formed balls into the powdered sugar and ensure they are well coated.

Place the coated dough balls about 1 inch (2.5 cm) apart on your prepared baking sheet. Gently press the tops of each to slightly flatten the top just a little.

Bake for 23 to 25 minutes, or until cracks begin to form and the bottoms are just barely beginning to turn golden brown. Remove from the oven and let cool on the baking sheet for a minute before transferring to a wire rack to cool completely.

Store in an airtight container for up to a week.

Rolled-Out Sugar Cookies

YIELDS APPROXIMATELY 30 COOKIES

Some sugar cookies are notorious for lacking in the flavor department. We counter this by adding a bit of cream cheese, which adds a tanginess that plays well with the vanilla while also making the cookie more tender. Although these are sugar cookies, they are vastly different from the drop sugar cookies in the previous chapter. Instead, they are formulated specifically to be able to make cutout cookies that retain their shape after baking, so that you may decorate them.

3 cups (375 g) all-purpose flour, plus more for dusting

1½ tsp (6 g) baking powder

½ tsp sea salt

1 cup (2 sticks/227 g) butter, at room temperature

2 oz (55 g) cream cheese, at room temperature

1 cup (200 g) granulated sugar

1 large egg, at room temperature

2 tsp (10 ml) vanilla extract

In a medium-sized bowl, whisk together the flour, baking powder and salt, then set aside. Have your favorite cookie cutters ready.

In the bowl of a stand mixer fitted with the paddle attachment, beat together the butter, cream cheese and sugar on medium speed until light and fluffy, about 5 minutes. Scrape down the sides and bottom of the bowl as needed.

Mix in the flour mixture until just combined, then turn out the dough onto a sheet of plastic wrap.

Shape the dough into an 8½ x 11–inch (21 x 28–cm) rectangle and cover tightly with the plastic wrap.

Chill the dough for at least an hour. Preheat the oven to 350°F (177°C) once the hour is up. Line two rimmed baking sheets with parchment paper or silicone baking mats.

Remove the dough from the refrigerator and remove the plastic wrap. On a lightly floured surface, roll out the dough into a larger rectangle that is about ¼ inch (6 mm) thick. If you get cracks in your dough, you can take a piece from the edge and press it down around the crack to patch it up. You don't want cracks when your cookie cutters are cutting, as they will show up on your final cookie.

Dip your cookie cutters in the surrounding flour, then cut out the shapes. Reroll the remaining dough as needed, and chill again if it begins to soften too much.

Place the cutouts at least 1 inch (2.5 cm) apart on the prepared baking sheets. Bake for 8 to 12 minutes, or until the edges are a light golden brown.

Remove from the oven and let cool on the baking sheet for 1 minute before transferring to a wire rack to cool completely.

Decorate as desired. You can use your favorite American buttercream frosting, royal icing or glazes. Finishing touches like sprinkles are also great!

Store in an airtight container for up to a week at room temperature.

Cinnamon Roll Cookies

YIELDS 24 COOKIES

I absolutely adore cinnamon rolls. It only makes sense to have them in cookie form, too. You also learn a fun way to add flavor and visual interest to your cookies with this flavor-packed swirl.

SWIRL

6 tbsp (85 g) unsalted butter, melted

⅓ cup (67 g) granulated sugar

⅓ cup (75 g) brown sugar

3 tbsp (23 g) all-purpose flour

3 tbsp (24 g) ground cinnamon

½ cup (57 g) toasted pecans, finely chopped

COOKIE DOUGH

2 cups (250 g) all-purpose flour, plus more for dusting

1 tsp sea salt

¼ tsp baking soda

½ cup (1 stick/114 g) unsalted butter, at room temperature

½ cup (100 g) granulated sugar

½ cup (110 g) brown sugar

1 large egg, at room temperature

2 tsp (10 ml) vanilla extract

GLAZE

2 tbsp (28 g) cream cheese, at room temperature

2 tbsp (28 g) unsalted butter, at room temperature

1 tsp vanilla extract

2½ cups (300 g) powdered sugar

1 to 2 tbsp (15 to 30 ml) heavy cream

Make the swirl: In a small saucepan, melt the butter over medium heat, then use a wooden spoon to stir in the granulated sugar, brown sugar, flour, cinnamon and chopped pecans. Set aside.

Make the cookie dough: In a medium-sized bowl, whisk together the flour, salt and baking soda, then set aside.

In the bowl of a stand mixer fitted with the paddle attachment, beat together the butter, granulated sugar and brown sugar on medium speed until light and fluffy, 4 to 5 minutes. Beat in the egg and vanilla until fully incorporated, 1 to 2 minutes.

Transfer the dough to a lightly floured surface and roll it out to an 8 x 14–inch (20 x 36–cm) rectangle. Trim the edges so they are straight and even.

Spread the cinnamon swirl mixture carefully over the dough. Leave a clean margin on both short sides and one longer side.

Roll the cookie dough into a log, starting with the longer side that doesn't have a clean margin. Make sure you roll the log tightly. Wrap the log with plastic wrap and chill for about 20 minutes in the freezer.

Preheat the oven to 350°F (177°C) as the dough chills. Line two baking sheets with parchment paper.

Slice the log crosswise into disks roughly ¼ inch (6 cm) thick, for best results, turning the log slightly after each slice, to keep each disk perfectly round.

Place the disks about 2 inches (5 cm) apart on the prepared baking sheets. Bake for 8 to 9 minutes, or until the edges are a light golden brown. Remove from the oven and allow to cool on the baking sheets for a minute before transferring to a wire rack to cool completely.

While the cookies are cooling, make the glaze: In a small bowl, using a balloon whisk, beat together the cream cheese, butter and vanilla until smooth. Add the powdered sugar, 1 cup (120 g) at a time, mixing it in thoroughly before adding the next cup. The mixture will get crumbly and this is normal.

Add the cream, 1 tablespoon (15 ml) at a time, mixing well as you do so.

Using a spoon, drizzle the glaze over the cooled cookies.

Store in an airtight container for up to a week at room temperature.

Lemony Spritz Cookies

YIELDS 70 COOKIES

Spritz cookies are a delightful cookie that is usually piped using a cookie press, but you can also use a piping bag and piping tip. I love how they hold their shape to create fun little morsels for you to bite into. This is the perfect recipe to practice your piping skills and getting the perfect dough consistency. Hint: This dough is meant to be silky smooth, for the best results.

SPECIAL EQUIPMENT

16-inch (40-cm) piping bag

Star piping tip

Cookie press (optional)

1 large egg yolk, at room temperature

1 tbsp (15 ml) heavy cream, at room temperature

1 tsp fresh lemon juice

½ tsp vanilla extract

1 cup (2 sticks/227 g) unsalted butter, at room temperature

⅔ cup (133 g) granulated sugar

2 tsp (4 g) lemon zest

½ tsp sea salt

2 cups (250 g) all-purpose flour

Preheat the oven to 375°F (191°C) and line two baking sheets with parchment paper or silicone baking mats.

In a small bowl, whisk together the egg yolk, cream, lemon juice and vanilla, then set aside.

In the bowl of a stand mixer fitted with the paddle attachment, beat together the butter, sugar, zest and salt on medium speed until light and fluffy, 4 to 5 minutes. Scrape down the sides and bottom of the bowl as needed.

Add the egg yolk mixture to the butter mixture, and beat until incorporated—this should take about another minute.

Add the flour and mix until just combined. You can chill the dough, covered with plastic wrap, up to a day in advance, but you must let the dough come to room temperature before using. This can take about an hour.

Fit a 16-inch (40-cm) piping bag with a star tip, or use a spritz cookie press, following the manufacturer's instructions. If using the piping bag method, hold the bag vertically directly over the prepared baking sheet and pipe a 1-inch (2.5-cm)-big dollop onto the lined pan, or swirl it to make a rosette. They should be at least 1½ inches (4 cm) apart.

Bake for 10 to 12 minutes, or until the edges are a golden brown. Remove from the oven and allow to cool on the baking sheet for a minute before transferring to a wire rack to cool completely.

Store in an airtight container at room temperature for up to 2 weeks.

Lovely Ladyfingers

YIELDS 28 COOKIES

Ladyfingers are a delicate, light and airy cookie that isn't often eaten on its own. They're great dipped in your coffee or tea, but are typically used to make other desserts, such as tiramisu. This recipe is a great way to practice whipping your egg whites and piping your dough.

SPECIAL EQUIPMENT
16-inch (40-cm) piping bag
Round piping tip

3 large eggs, separated
¼ cup (50 g) granulated sugar, divided
1 tsp vanilla extract
½ cup (60 g) cake flour, sifted
Powdered sugar, for dusting

Preheat the oven to 350°F (177°C). Line two baking sheets with parchment paper or silicone baking mats.

In a large bowl, whisk together the egg yolks and 2 tablespoons (26 g) of the sugar until the mixture is thick and pale yellow, about 5 minutes. Add the vanilla and whisk well for another minute.

Place a fine-mesh strainer over the bowl, sift in the cake flour, then set the bowl aside without stirring.

In the bowl of a stand mixer fitted with the whisk attachment, beat together the egg whites and the remaining 2 tablespoons (26 g) of granulated sugar on medium speed until stiff peaks form. This is when the egg whites stand up straight when you remove your whisk and hold it upside down.

Fold the egg whites into the egg yolk mixture, using a rubber spatula to gently incorporate everything.

Fit a 16-inch (40-cm) piping bag with a round tip and fill with the batter. Pipe 3-inch (8-cm)-long logs, 1 inch (2.5 cm) apart, onto your prepared baking sheets.

Dust the piped logs with powdered sugar, then bake for 8 to 10 minutes, or until the edges are a pale golden brown. Remove from the oven and let cool on the baking sheets for 3 to 4 minutes before transferring to a wire rack to cool completely.

Store in an airtight container in the freezer for up to a month. Thaw at room temperature.

The Greatest Gingerbread

YIELDS APPROXIMATELY 30 COOKIES

Gingerbread is so much fun. You will want to learn this recipe for the holidays because this dough can be used to make gingerbread houses, people and even those cute little mug decorations. It doesn't spread, doesn't get puffy and is sturdy enough for any creative bakes, while still being tender and delicious enough to eat as is. I like my gingerbread forward on the ginger and to let the other spices fall back more to play supporting roles, to amplify that ginger flavor.

3 cups (375 g) all-purpose flour, plus more for dusting

1 tsp baking soda

2½ tsp (2 g) ground ginger

2 tsp (5 g) ground cinnamon

¼ tsp freshly ground black pepper

¼ tsp ground nutmeg

¼ tsp ground allspice

½ tsp sea salt

½ cup (1 stick/114 g) unsalted butter, at room temperature

⅔ cup (147 g) light brown sugar

⅔ cup (226 g) molasses

1 large egg, at room temperature

1 tsp vanilla extract

In a medium-sized bowl, whisk together the flour, baking soda, ginger, cinnamon, pepper, nutmeg, allspice and salt, then set aside.

In the bowl of a stand mixer fitted with the paddle attachment, beat together the butter and brown sugar on medium speed until light and fluffy, 3 to 5 minutes.

Beat the molasses into the butter mixture for 2 minutes, or until fully incorporated. Scrape down the sides and bottom of the bowl as needed.

Add the egg and vanilla, then mix for another minute, or until well combined.

Mix in the flour on low speed until just incorporated. Turn out the dough onto a sheet of plastic wrap and form into a disk. Wrap tightly in the plastic wrap, then chill for at least 1 hour, preferably overnight to develop the flavors.

Preheat the oven to 350°F (177°C). Line two rimmed baking sheets with parchment paper or silicone baking mats. Set aside.

Unwrap the dough and transfer to a lightly floured surface, then roll out until it is about ¼ inch (6 mm) thick. If you get cracks in your dough, you can take a piece from the edge and press it down around the crack to patch it up. Lightly flour a cookie cutter and cut out shapes.

Place the cutouts about 1 inch (2.5 cm) apart on your prepared baking sheets (you will be baking these cookies in batches). You can reroll the scraps to make more cookies. If the leftover dough gets too soft, you can rewrap it and refrigerate for another 30 minutes before rolling out again.

Bake for 8 to 10 minutes, or until the edges are a nice golden brown. Remove from the oven and let cool on the baking sheets for 2 minutes before transferring to a wire rack to cool completely.

Store in an airtight container for up to 2 weeks at room temperature.

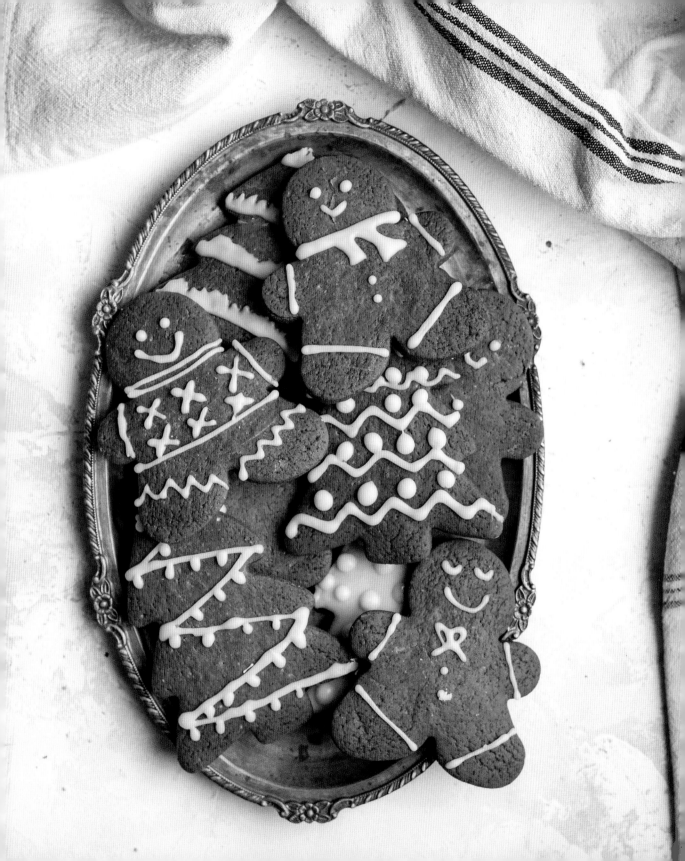

Birthday Girl Snowball Cookies

YIELDS 18 COOKIES

I don't like celebrating my birthday, but I never say no to some Birthday Girl Snowball Cookies. I love how buttery and fun these are. You can mimic the taste of that classic boxed birthday cake flavor from your childhood by using cake batter–flavored extract, which can be found in most well-stocked grocery or craft stores. The almond helps to amplify that cake flavor.

2½ cups (313 g) all-purpose flour

⅓ cup (33 g) almond flour

¼ tsp sea salt

½ cup (96 g) sprinkles, divided

1 cup (2 sticks/227 g) unsalted butter, at room temperature

⅓ cup (67 g) granulated sugar

1 tsp cake batter extract

½ tsp vanilla extract

1½ cups (180 g) powdered sugar

Preheat the oven to 325°F (163°C). Line two rimmed baking sheets with parchment paper or silicone baking mats.

In a medium-sized bowl, whisk together the flour, almond flour, salt and ⅓ cup (64 g) of the sprinkles, then set aside.

In the bowl of a stand mixer fitted with the paddle attachment, beat together the butter and granulated sugar on medium speed until light and fluffy, about 3 minutes.

Add the cake batter extract and vanilla to the butter mixture and mix until well combined, scraping the sides and bottom of the mixing bowl as needed.

Mix in the flour mixture until everything comes together. The mixture may look clumpy, but it will stick together when you press it together with your hands, which is what you want.

Divide the dough into balls that are 2 tablespoons (1¾ inches [4.5 cm] or 47 g) big, then place them 2 inches (5 cm) apart on the prepared baking sheets.

Bake for 13 to 15 minutes, or until the cookies are starting to brown along the sides, then remove them from the oven.

Remove from the oven and allow to cool on the baking sheets until they are just cool enough to touch.

Take the remaining 2⅔ tablespoons (32 g) of sprinkles and lightly crush them, then, in a small bowl, stir them into the powdered sugar.

Toss the warm cookies in the bowl of the powdered sugar mixture until completely coated. Leave them on a wire rack to cool completely, then toss in the powdered sugar mixture again.

Store the cookies in an airtight container at room temperature for up to a week.

Perfectly Spiced Speculoos Cookies

YIELDS APPROXIMATELY 15 COOKIES

Speculoos, a Belgium spice cookie, are one of my favorite cutout cookies to make. They're simple and delicate in flavor, but so comforting. And if you've heard of cookie butter, you might be delighted to hear that it's frequently made with speculoos cookies.

1⅔ cups (208 g) all-purpose flour, plus more for dusting

2 tsp (5 g) ground cinnamon

¼ tsp sea salt

¼ tsp baking soda

⅛ tsp ground cloves

7 tbsp (99 g) unsalted butter, at room temperature

½ cup (100 g) granulated sugar

½ cup (110 g) dark brown sugar

1 large egg, at room temperature

In a medium-sized bowl, whisk together the flour, cinnamon, salt, baking soda and cloves, then set aside.

In the bowl of a stand mixer fitted with the paddle attachment, beat together the butter, granulated sugar and brown sugar on medium speed until light and fluffy, about 5 minutes.

Add the egg to the butter mixture and beat well for another 2 minutes, scraping down the sides and bottom of the bowl as needed.

Gradually add the flour mixture while mixing on low speed, until just combined. Turn out the dough onto a sheet of plastic wrap and shape into an 8 x 10–inch (20 x 25–cm) rectangle. Wrap tightly in the plastic wrap and chill for at least 3 hours, preferably overnight to develop the flavors.

Preheat the oven to 350°F (177°C). Line two rimmed baking sheets with parchment paper or silicone baking mats.

Unwrap the dough and transfer to a lightly floured surface. Roll out until it is about ¼ inch (6 mm) thick, then use lightly floured cookie cutters to cut out shapes. Reroll the cookie dough as needed. If the leftover dough starts to feel soft, wrap in plastic wrap and refrigerate for about 30 minutes before rolling out again.

Place the cutouts 1 inch (2.5 cm) apart on your prepared baking sheets and bake for 8 to 10 minutes, or until they are lightly golden brown.

Remove from the oven and leave the cookies on the baking sheet for about 2 minutes before transferring to a wire rack to cool completely.

Store in an airtight container for up to 2 weeks at room temperature.

Vanilla Biscotti

YIELDS 34 COOKIES

Biscotti are Italian twice-baked cookies that are traditionally served with coffee or espresso. I love vanilla biscotti because they are the perfect canvas for adding flavors. Master this base recipe, and you are already more than halfway there to a million types of biscotti. It might seem like messy work forming the dough into logs but flour your hands and you'll be fine!

2¼ cups (281 g) all-purpose flour

1½ tsp (6 g) baking powder

½ tsp sea salt

6 tbsp (85 g) unsalted butter, at room temperature

¾ cup (150 g) granulated sugar

2 large eggs, at room temperature

1 tbsp (15 ml) vanilla extract

6 oz (170 g) white chocolate (optional)

Extra Credit: *You can add 1 to 2 teaspoons (2 to 4 g) of any type of zest into the biscotti dough, as well as ½ cup (about 75 g) of nuts or dried fruits. Chocolate chips make a tasty addition, and so do a number of spices. Have fun mixing and matching!*

Preheat the oven to 350°F (177°C). Line one or two baking sheets with parchment paper.

In a medium-sized bowl, whisk together the flour, baking powder and salt, then set aside.

In the bowl of a stand mixer fitted with the paddle attachment, beat together the butter and sugar on medium speed until light and fluffy, about 3 minutes.

Add the eggs and vanilla to the butter mixture, then beat until well combined, about 2 minutes. Scrape down the sides and bottom of the bowl as needed.

Gradually add the flour mixture while mixing on low speed, until just incorporated.

Turn out the dough onto a lightly floured surface and divide into two portions. The dough may be sticky, so flour your hands when handling.

Shape each portion into a 2 x 11–inch (5 x 28–cm) log. Place each log on the prepared baking sheet. You can fit two logs on one baking sheet as long as there are a few inches (at least 5 cm) between the logs, or you can put each on its own prepared pan.

Bake for 25 minutes, then remove from the oven. Use a serrated knife to cut the logs crosswise into pieces ½ to ¾ inch (1.3 to 2 cm) thick. A serrated knife is important to use because the grooves ensure a cleaner and easier cut without needing to apply a lot of pressure on the logs. Lay them ¼ inch (6 mm) apart, cut side down, back on their lined pans, then bake for another 10 minutes. They should be only lightly golden brown.

Remove from the oven and transfer the biscotti to a wire rack to cool completely. They will harden as they cool.

In a microwave-safe bowl, microwave the white chocolate (if using) for 20 seconds. Remove from the microwave and stir well. Microwave again for 20 seconds more, and stir again. Repeat until melted. Be careful not to overheat, as white chocolate is more temperamental and likely to seize (become stiff).

Dip the cooled biscotti into the melted chocolate.

Store in an airtight container for up to a month at room temperature.

Brownie Biscotti

YIELDS 28 COOKIES

These biscotti are not shy with the chocolate flavor. They smell amazing and taste even better. Dust your hands with cocoa powder if you have trouble handling the dough, and don't forget to use a serrated knife for clean cuts!

2 cups (250 g) all-purpose flour

½ cup (42 g) unsweetened cocoa powder, plus more for dusting

¾ tsp baking soda

½ tsp baking powder

¼ tsp sea salt

½ cup (1 stick/114 g) unsalted butter, at room temperature

1 cup (200 g) granulated sugar

2 large eggs, at room temperature

1 tsp pure vanilla extract

¾ cup (130 g) chopped chocolate

2 tbsp (25 g) turbinado sugar, for topping

Preheat the oven to 350°F (177°C) and line one or two baking sheets with parchment paper or silicone baking mats.

In a medium-sized bowl, whisk together the flour, cocoa powder, baking soda, baking powder and salt, then set aside.

In the bowl of a stand mixer fitted with the paddle attachment, beat together the butter and granulated sugar on medium speed until light and fluffy, about 4 minutes.

One at a time, beat the eggs into the butter mixture, then add the vanilla. Scrape down the sides and bottom of the bowl as needed.

Stir in the flour mixture and mix just until the dough starts to come together, then add the chopped chocolate.

Turn out the dough onto a parchment-lined surface that is lightly dusted with cocoa powder. Mix the dough together if there are any bits of flour not mixed in.

Divide the dough equally into two portions and shape them into 2- to 3-inch (5- to 8-cm) x 12-inch (30-cm) logs. You may need to dust your hands with cocoa powder if your dough feels a little sticky. It can be a messy process, but it's worth it!

Space the logs generously apart (at least 3 inches [8 cm]) on one prepared baking sheet because they will spread. Alternatively, you can use two baking sheets to bake them.

Sprinkle the tops of the logs lightly with turbinado sugar and bake for 25 minutes, turning after the first 10 minutes of baking.

Remove from the oven, leaving the oven on. Use a serrated knife to gently cut the logs crosswise into pieces that are about ½ inch (1.3 cm) thick.

Place the cookies ¼ inch (6 mm) apart, cut side down, back on their lined pan, and bake for an additional 10 minutes, turning halfway through.

Remove from the oven and allow to cool on the baking sheet for about 2 minutes before transferring to a wire rack to cool completely.

Store in an airtight container for up to a month at room temperature.

Gingerbread Biscotti

YIELDS 38 COOKIES

It's no secret that gingerbread is one of my favorite holiday flavors, so I needed to include this Gingerbread Biscotti in the book. I love this recipe because it really shows how it only takes simple spices to make a big flavor impact. You can also see how we can make slight adjustments to the ingredients to be able to include some molasses for that signature depth of flavor we expect from gingerbread.

2½ cups (313 g) all-purpose flour, plus more for dusting

2½ tsp (5 g) ground ginger

1 tsp ground cinnamon

¼ tsp ground cloves

¼ tsp ground allspice

¼ tsp freshly ground black pepper

1½ tsp (6 g) baking powder

½ tsp sea salt

5 tbsp (71 g) unsalted butter, at room temperature

¾ cup (165 g) dark brown sugar

2 large eggs, at room temperature

3 tbsp (60 g) molasses

1 tsp vanilla extract

Preheat the oven to 350°F (177°C). Line a baking sheet or two with parchment paper and set aside.

In a medium-sized bowl, whisk together the flour, ginger, cinnamon, cloves, allspice, pepper, baking powder and salt, then set aside.

In the bowl of a stand mixer fitted with the paddle attachment, beat together the butter and brown sugar on medium speed until light and fluffy, about 4 minutes.

Mix the eggs, molasses and vanilla into the butter mixture, then beat until fully incorporated, another 2 to 3 minutes. Scrape down the sides and bottom of the bowl as needed.

Add the flour mixture and mix until just combined.

Turn out the dough onto a lightly floured surface and divide into two equal portions. Shape each into a 2 x 11–inch (5 x 28–cm) log.

Place them a few inches (about 5 cm) apart on your prepared baking sheet, or you can put them on separate baking sheets.

Bake for 25 minutes, then remove from the oven. Cut the logs crosswise into pieces ½ to ¾ inch (1.3 to 2 cm) thick. Place the slices ¼ inch (6 cm) apart, cut side down, back on their baking sheet and bake for an additional 10 minutes. There shouldn't be a big visual difference when they're finished baking.

Remove from the oven and allow to cool on the baking sheet for about 5 minutes before transferring to a wire rack to cool completely.

Store in an airtight container for up to a month at room temperature.

Junior Cookies

Sandwiched and Stuffed

In my opinion, cookies are so much more fun when you add a little extra to the party. Stuffing cookies with a surprise filling, such as my favorite Gotta Have Brown Butter Brownie-Stuffed Cookies (page 93), or sandwiching them, such as the unforgettable Apple Pie Cookies (page 119), is a delicious way to add more flavor and/or texture. It also allows you more room to explore different flavor combinations.

I always say the only limits are your own imagination, and that's never been truer than with this type of cookie. You can add jams, frostings, nuts, streusel, curds and so much more to your cookies. Think of all the delicious things you can do to the cookie itself, and you will never run out of different cookies to bake up and share.

The trick to making a good stuffed cookie is to pay attention to the temperatures and chilling times. You will often find that your filling needs to be very cold to handle and work into the middle of the dough. This means you might have to work in small batches or take time to let your filling chill again before continuing your assembly. These take practice, but mostly patience—and a willingness to get your hands a little messy! The end product is always worth it.

Gotta Have Brown Butter Brownie-Stuffed Cookies

YIELDS 24 COOKIES

These cookies are pretty rich and decadent with their delicious brownie center. I like to take things up a notch with the small twist of using brown butter, a technique we practiced in the earlier chapters, to add more depth and nuttiness to the party. It does take some work to make this cookie, so you can make the brownie filling up to a day in advance.

BROWNIE FILLING

6 tbsp (85 g) unsalted butter

½ cup (63 g) all-purpose flour

3 tbsp (15 g) unsweetened cocoa powder

¼ tsp sea salt

⅔ cup (115 g) chopped semisweet chocolate or chips

½ cup (100 g) granulated sugar

1 tsp vanilla extract

1 large egg, at room temperature

CHOCOLATE CHIP COOKIE DOUGH

1 cup (2 sticks/227 g) unsalted butter, at room temperature

2½ cups (313 g) all-purpose flour

1 tsp cornstarch

1 tsp baking soda

¾ tsp sea salt

1 cup (220 g) brown sugar

¾ cup (150 g) granulated sugar

1 large egg, at room temperature

1 large egg yolk, at room temperature

2½ tsp (12 ml) vanilla extract

1½ cups (255 g) chocolate chips

Make the brownie filling: In a medium-sized saucepan, heat the butter over medium heat, stirring frequently until it is browned and smells nutty. Immediately remove the butter from the heat and leave it in the pan. (You can also brown the butter for the chocolate chip cookie dough at the same time, using a separate saucepan, and store that in a container in the refrigerator until mostly, but not completely, resolidified.)

In a small bowl, whisk together the flour, cocoa powder and salt, then set aside.

Add the semisweet chocolate to the still-hot saucepan of brown butter. Stir until the chocolate is melted and combined with the butter. Stir in the granulated sugar.

Allow the mixture to cool slightly before adding the vanilla and egg. Stir well until fully combined.

Fold the butter and chocolate mixture into the flour mixture and stir until there are no streaks of flour. Transfer the brownie batter to the refrigerator to cool and harden.

Make the cookie dough: If you haven't already done so, brown the butter as described in the first step of the brownie filling instructions and remove it from the heat, or else remove the chilled brown butter from the refrigerator.

In a medium-sized bowl, whisk together the flour, cornstarch, baking soda and salt, then set aside.

In the bowl of a stand mixer fitted with the whisk attachment, beat together the brown butter, brown sugar and granulated sugar on medium speed until the mixture is light and fluffy, about 5 minutes.

Beat the egg and egg yolk into the butter mixture until well combined. Scrape down the sides and bottom of the bowl and beat in the vanilla.

(continued)

Gotta Have Brown Butter Brownie-Stuffed Cookies (Continued)

Mix in the flour mixture until there are no more streaks of flour showing, then fold in the chocolate chips.

Chill the dough for at least an hour, preferably overnight.

Remove the dough and brownie batter from the refrigerator and then preheat the oven to 350°F (177°C). Line two baking sheets with parchment paper or silicone baking mats.

Take 2 tablespoons (1¾ inches [4.5 cm] in diameter or 49 g) of the cookie dough and flatten it into a disk. Take a generous 1½ teaspoons (¾ inch [2 cm] in diameter, or 9 g) of the brownie batter and roll it into a ball. Place the ball on the center of the cookie dough disk. Wrap the cookie dough around the brownie batter and shape it into a ball. Repeat with all the remaining dough and brownie batter.

Place the filled dough balls 2 inches (5 cm) apart on the prepared baking sheets.

Bake for 12 to 14 minutes, or until the edges are set and a light golden brown.

Remove the cookies from the oven and allow them to cool on the baking sheet for 2 to 3 minutes, then transfer them to a wire rack to cool completely.

Store the cookies in an airtight container for up to a week at room temperature.

Chocoholic's Chocolate Hazelnut-Stuffed Chocolate Snickerdoodles

YIELDS ABOUT 25 COOKIES

I get chocolate cravings that require an intense chocolate punch. These cookies are just that. I love them because we also test our skills by making homemade Nutella®. You can buy some in a pinch, but this recipe is just too good to pass up. The recipe for the spread can be made a day or two in advance, but be careful not to eat it all before you need it; you will have some extra left over after making the cookies. It really tests your patience and ability to work quickly because the spread thaws quickly.

CHOCOLATE HAZELNUT SPREAD

1 cup (142 g) raw hazelnuts

1 cup (120 g) powdered sugar

⅓ cup (28 g) unsweetened cocoa powder

2 tbsp (30 ml) canola oil

1 tsp vanilla extract

¼ tsp sea salt

4 oz (115 g) semisweet chocolate

2 to 3 tbsp (30 to 45 ml) heavy cream, or as needed

Make the chocolate hazelnut spread: Preheat the oven to 350°F (177°C). Place your hazelnuts on a rimmed baking sheet and roast in the oven for 12 minutes, or until you can smell them and the skins look as if they're peeling away on some of them.

Remove from the oven and let the hazelnuts cool just enough for you to be able to handle them. Pour them out onto a clean kitchen towel and rub them with the towel. This will help remove the skins. You can use your hand to remove some of the more stubborn pieces of skin, but leaving some skins on is okay as long as most of them are removed.

In a food processor, pulse the hazelnuts until they form a fine powder. Add the powdered sugar and cocoa powder and pulse well.

Drizzle in the oil and vanilla, then pulse until the mixture forms a thick paste.

In a microwave-safe bowl, microwave the chocolate for 30 seconds, then remove from the microwave and stir well. Microwave for another 30 seconds and stir well again. If there are still bits of unmelted chocolate, microwave for another 15 seconds and stir well. Add the melted chocolate to the hazelnut mixture in the food processor and pulse until smooth.

Check the consistency of the mixture. If it seems too thick, add the cream, 1 tablespoon (15 ml) at a time, to get a spreadable consistency. If making ahead of time, store in an airtight container in the refrigerator.

(continued)

CHOCOLATE SNICKERDOODLES

2¼ cups (281 g) all-purpose flour

⅔ cup (56 g) natural unsweetened cocoa powder

1½ tsp (5 g) cream of tartar

1 tsp baking soda

½ tsp sea salt

1 cup (227 g) unsalted butter, at room temperature

1 cup (220 g) light brown sugar

1 cup (200 g) granulated sugar, divided

2 large eggs, at room temperature

2 tsp (10 ml) vanilla extract

Make the snickerdoodles: In a medium-sized bowl, whisk together the flour, cocoa powder, cream of tartar, baking soda and salt, then set aside.

In the bowl of a stand mixer fitted with the paddle attachment, beat together the butter, brown sugar and ¾ cup (150 g) of the granulated sugar on medium speed for 4 to 5 minutes, or until light and fluffy.

Add the eggs and vanilla to the butter mixture, and beat on medium speed until incorporated, at least another 2 to 3 minutes. Scrape down the sides and bottom of the bowl as needed.

Stir in the flour mixture and beat on low speed until just combined. Cover the dough with plastic wrap and chill for at least an hour.

Portion the chocolate hazelnut spread into 1½-teaspoon (9-g) dollops and place onto a parchment paper–lined baking sheet and freeze.

Preheat the oven to 350°F (177°C) and line two rimmed baking sheets with parchment paper or silicone baking mats. Place the remaining ¼ cup (50 g) of the granulated sugar in a bowl.

Remove the cookie dough from the refrigerator and portion the dough into balls about 2 tablespoons (1¾ inches [4.5 cm] or 45 g) big. Create an indentation in each ball, then fill with a frozen dollop of the frozen chocolate hazelnut spread, then cover with the dough and re-form into a ball. The spread thaws quickly, so it is best to keep it in the freezer as you assemble each ball of cookie dough.

Roll the stuffed dough balls in the bowl of granulated sugar. Place them at least 2 inches (5 cm) apart on the prepared baking sheets. Bake for 8 to 10 minutes, or until they are puffed and the edges look set.

Remove from the oven and allow the cookies to cool on the baking sheets for at least 4 minutes before transferring to a wire rack to cool completely.

Store in an airtight container for up to a week at room temperature.

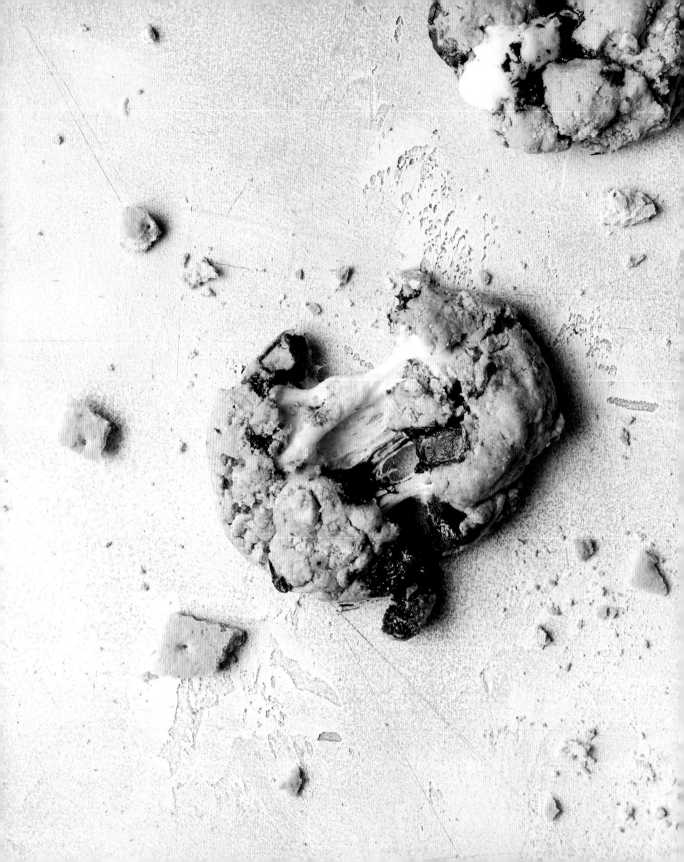

Magical Peanut Butter S'mores

YIELDS 24 COOKIES

These cookies are soft, chewy and peanut buttery! They have a delicious marshmallow center that makes these a sweet mess you can't get enough of. For the perfect cookies, you need to be patient with multiple chillings and baking a few cookies at a time. I like to use halved marshmallows in this recipe; you can try using a whole marshmallow, but I recommend freezing them to make it easier to wrap up in the cookie dough. And be prepared for a few tasty cookie explosions. These cookies are baked in smaller batches for the best results.

2½ cups (312 g) all-purpose flour

1 tsp baking soda

1 tsp baking powder

1 tsp sea salt

½ cup (1 stick/114 g) unsalted butter

¾ cup (192 g) creamy peanut butter

½ cup (110 g) granulated sugar

1 cup (220 g) packed dark brown sugar

2 large eggs, at room temperature

1 large egg yolk, at room temperature

2 tsp (10 ml) vanilla extract

⅓ cup (48 g) roasted peanuts, finely chopped

1 cup (90 g) crushed cinnamon graham crackers

2 cups (340 g) semisweet chocolate chips

12 large marshmallows

In a medium-sized bowl, whisk together the flour, baking soda, baking powder and salt, then set aside.

In the bowl of a stand mixer fitted with the paddle attachment, beat together the butter, peanut butter, granulated sugar and brown sugar on medium speed until light and fluffy, about 5 minutes.

Add the eggs, egg yolk and vanilla to the butter mixture, and beat on medium speed until well incorporated—this should take 2 to 3 minutes. Scrape down the sides and bottom of the bowl as needed.

Gradually add the flour mixture while mixing on low speed, until just combined. Fold in the peanuts, crushed graham crackers and chocolate chips.

Cover the dough with plastic wrap and chill for at least 30 minutes. Halve the marshmallows. Remove the cookie dough and portion it into balls about 2 tablespoons (1¾ inches [4.5 cm] or 49 g) big. Flatten them and place a halved marshmallow on the center of each disk of flattened dough, then wrap the dough around the marshmallow and roll into a ball.

Place the dough on a baking sheet and chill it again for at least another 30 minutes, but no longer than an hour.

Preheat the oven to 350°F (177°C). Line a baking sheet with parchment paper or a silicone baking mat.

Place six filled dough balls 2 inches (5 cm) apart on the prepared baking sheet and bake for 10 minutes, or until the edges are set and a nice golden brown, and the cookies are puffy. If the cookie separates from the marshmallow at all, you can use a spatula to gently press it back onto the marshmallow while everything is still hot.

Remove from the oven and allow them to cool on the baking sheet for 2 to 3 minutes before transferring to a wire rack.

Store in an airtight container for up to 3 days at room temperature.

Mocha Cookies for Coffee Lovers

YIELDS 10 SANDWICH COOKIES

This cookie has the perfect balance of coffee and chocolate together and is delightfully rich. It's simple to make, which means it's the perfect recipe for an introduction to putting together a tasty sandwich cookie.

COOKIE DOUGH

¾ cup (94 g) all-purpose flour

¾ cup (63 g) Dutch-processed cocoa powder

2 tbsp (20 g) instant coffee granules

1 tsp baking powder

½ tsp sea salt

½ cup (1 stick/114 g) unsalted butter, at room temperature

1 cup (220 g) light brown sugar

1 large egg, at room temperature

1 tsp vanilla extract

FILLING

½ cup (1 stick/114 g) unsalted butter, at room temperature

1½ cups (180 g) powdered sugar

2 tbsp (10 g) unsweetened cocoa powder

3 tbsp (42 g) heavy cream

3 tbsp (30 g) instant coffee granules

Make the cookie dough: Preheat the oven to 350°F (177°C). Line two baking sheets with parchment paper or silicone baking mats.

In a medium-sized bowl, whisk together the flour, cocoa powder, coffee granules, baking powder and salt, then set aside.

In the bowl of a stand mixer fitted with the paddle attachment, beat together the butter and brown sugar on medium speed until light and fluffy, 4 to 5 minutes.

Scrape down the sides and bottom of the bowl, then add the egg and vanilla to the butter mixture. Beat again on medium speed for another 3 minutes to fully incorporate.

Add the flour mixture and mix on low speed until just combined and there are no streaks of flour.

Portion the dough into balls that are 1½ tablespoons (1½ inches [4 cm] or 32 g) big and slightly flatten the top of each. Place them at least 2 inches (5 cm) apart on the prepared baking sheets.

Bake for 8 to 9 minutes, or until the edges look set and the cookies have puffed in the center.

Remove from the oven and allow to cool on the baking sheet for 2 to 3 minutes before transferring to a wire rack to cool completely.

Make the filling: In a small bowl, with a balloon whisk, beat the butter until smooth, then add the powdered sugar and cocoa powder. Mix until well combined. The mixture will likely look lumpy—this is normal.

In a small saucepan, heat the cream over medium-low heat for only a few seconds to gently warm it enough to mix in and dissolve the instant coffee granules. Let the mixture cool completely to room temperature. Drizzle the mixture into the filling mixture, stirring, until it reaches a smooth, spreadable consistency.

Turn half of the cooled cookies upside down, then spread some of the filling onto the bottom of the cookies. Top with the remaining cookies (right side up) to sandwich them.

Store in an airtight container for up to 3 days at room temperature.

Milk's Favorite Cookie-Stuffed Peanut Butter Cookies

YIELDS 18 COOKIES

Ever since seeing the 1998 version of The Parent Trap, *where Lindsay Lohan's characters dip their Oreos in peanut butter, I've loved that combination of flavors. These are pretty amazing, especially if you melt some peanut butter chips, drizzle it on top of the cookies and top with more cookie crumbs.*

1¼ cups (156 g) all-purpose flour

½ tsp baking soda

¼ tsp sea salt

½ cup (1 stick/114 g) unsalted butter, at room temperature

½ cup (110 g) dark brown sugar

⅓ cup (67 g) granulated sugar

1 large egg, at room temperature

¾ cup (192 g) creamy peanut butter

1 tsp vanilla extract

22 mini chocolate sandwich cookies, such as Oreos, divided

½ cup (85 g) peanut butter chips

In a medium-sized bowl, whisk together the flour, baking soda and salt, then set aside.

In the bowl of a stand mixer fitted with the paddle attachment, beat together the butter, brown sugar and granulated sugar on medium speed for 4 to 5 minutes, or until light and fluffy.

Add the egg, peanut butter and vanilla to the butter mixture and beat on medium speed for another 3 to 4 minutes, or until well combined. Scrape down the sides and bottom of the bowl as needed. Stir in the flour mixture until just incorporated and there are no streaks of flour.

Cover the dough with plastic wrap and chill for at least 30 minutes, or until the dough is easy to handle.

Portion the dough into balls 1½ tablespoons (1½ inches [4 cm] or 35 g) big. Create a deep indentation and insert a mini cookie. Cover with the surrounding dough so the mini cookie is no longer visible and re-form into a ball.

Place the stuffed dough balls on a baking sheet lined with parchment paper or a silicone baking mat. Keep the dough balls refrigerated as you preheat the oven to 350°F (177°C) and line another baking sheet for a total of two prepared baking sheets.

Separate the cookie dough balls so they are at least 2 inches (5 cm) apart, placing half of them on the second lined pan. Bake for 10 to 12 minutes, or until the edges are golden brown and the cookies are puffed.

Remove from the oven and allow to cool on the baking sheets for 2 minutes before transferring to a wire rack to cool completely.

In a microwave-safe bowl, microwave the peanut butter chips for 30 seconds, then remove from the microwave and stir well. Microwave for another 15 seconds, if needed, and stir well again. Continue to microwave in 15-second bursts, stirring well after each, until the chips are completely melted.

Drizzle the melted peanut butter chips on the cookies. Crush the remaining mini cookies and sprinkle over the peanut butter drizzle.

Store in an airtight container for up to a week at room temperature.

Better-Than-Store-Bought Double Chocolate Sandwich Cookies

YIELDS 20 COOKIES

My homemade Milanos® are a favorite on my website. I always wondered why there isn't a commercial version of my full-on chocolate version. As it turns out, just a few adjustments gives us a chocoholic's dream. Even pressure and holding your piping bag directly over the baking sheet helps get you perfect, even rounds every time. This makes great practice for more advanced cookies, such as macarons (page 144).

SPECIAL EQUIPMENT

16-inch (40-cm) piping bag

Large round piping tip

COOKIE DOUGH

¾ cup (94 g) all-purpose flour

½ cup (42 g) Dutch-processed cocoa powder

½ tsp sea salt

½ cup (1 stick/114 g) unsalted butter, at room temperature

1¼ cups (168 g) powdered sugar

1 large egg white, at room temperature

1 large egg, at room temperature

1 tsp vanilla extract

1½ tbsp (22 ml) brewed coffee, at room temperature

Preheat the oven to 350°F (177°C). Line two baking sheets with parchment paper or silicone baking mats. Set aside.

In a small bowl, stir together the flour, cocoa powder and salt, then set aside.

In the bowl of a stand mixer fitted with the paddle attachment, beat together the butter and powdered sugar on medium speed until light in color, about 4 minutes. Scrape down the sides and bottom of your bowl.

Add the egg white and whole egg to the butter mixture, and beat on medium speed for about 2 minutes. Add the vanilla and coffee, and beat on medium speed for about 2 additional minutes, or until the mixture is well combined. Scrape down the sides and bottom of the bowl as needed.

Gradually add the flour mixture while mixing on low speed, until just incorporated. Alternatively, you can use a spatula to slowly stir in the flour mixture.

Fit a large round piping tip into a 16-inch (40-cm) piping bag. Bend the bottom of the piping bag so the tip is facing upward and place the bag in a tall cup. Fold down the top of the piping bag over the lip of the glass.

Use a spoon or spring-trigger ice-cream scoop to fill the piping bag with the batter. You want to only partially fill the bag. Most disposable piping bags will have a guideline where they recommend you stop filling the bag.

Lift the bag out of the cup and twist the top of the bag to push the batter down toward the tip and close off the top.

Hold the piping bag with one hand at the top of the bag, and your other hand down closer to the tip of the bag.

(continued)

Better-Than-Store-Bought Double Chocolate Sandwich Cookies (Continued)

CHOCOLATE FILLING

1 cup (170 g) chopped dark chocolate

2 tbsp (30 ml) heavy cream

Keeping the bag vertical above your baking pan, pipe the dough onto the liner sheet into 2-inch (5-cm) logs that are about 2 inches (5 cm) apart. If you have tails from the piping, you can use a lightly moistened finger to pat them down into the batter.

Bake the cookies for 14 to 16 minutes, or until they look set. The edges should feel crisp, but the tops should still feel a little soft. Remove from the oven and allow them to cool on the baking sheet for 2 minutes before transferring to a wire rack to cool completely.

Melt the chocolate: In a microwave-safe bowl, combine the chocolate and cream and microwave for 30 seconds. Remove from the microwave and stir well. Microwave for another 20 seconds and stir well again. If the chocolate is still not fully melted, place in the microwave for another 20 seconds and stir well again. You may repeat this one more time if any chocolate has still not melted. Stir the mixture until it is fully combined.

Turn half of the cookies bottom up. Use a spoon to spread the chocolate on the upturned bottoms, and sandwich them with the remaining (right side up) cookies. Allow them to set at room temperature.

Store in an airtight container for up to a week at room temperature.

The Best Caramel-Stuffed Brown Butter Pumpkin Cookies

YIELDS 22 COOKIES

These cookies are good enough to make the most adamant pumpkin spice hater into a total pumpkin spice lover. These are best when they're fresh and set just enough for you to be able to handle them. It makes great practice for browning butter (and seeing how well it plays with spices!) and paying attention to stuffing cookies with caramel, which can be messy work if not done well.

1 cup (2 sticks/227 g) unsalted butter

1¾ cups (219 g) all-purpose flour

1 tbsp (10 g) pumpkin pie spice

½ tsp baking soda

½ tsp baking powder

½ tsp sea salt

1 cup (220 g) light brown sugar

2 large egg yolks, at room temperature

2 tsp (10 ml) vanilla extract

½ cup (122 g) pure pumpkin puree, at room temperature

22 soft caramel candies

½ cup (100 g) granulated sugar, for rolling

1 tsp ground cinnamon, for rolling

In a small saucepan, heat your butter over medium heat, stirring frequently, until it fully melts and begins to smell nutty.

Remove from the heat and transfer the brown butter to a heatproof container. Store in the refrigerator (or freezer if you're in a hurry) until the butter is a little over halfway solidified.

In a medium-sized bowl, whisk together your flour, pumpkin spice, baking soda, baking powder and salt, then set aside.

In the bowl of a stand mixer fitted with the paddle attachment, beat the brown butter on medium speed until light and fluffy, about 3 minutes. Add the egg yolks, vanilla and pumpkin puree. Scrape down the sides and bottom of the bowl as needed. Beat until the ingredients are fully incorporated; this should take another 2 to 3 minutes.

Gradually add the flour mixture while mixing on low speed, until just combined and there are no streaks of flour.

Cover the dough with plastic wrap and chill for at least 30 minutes, preferably overnight for the best flavor.

Remove the cookie dough from the refrigerator and portion it into balls that are about 1½ tablespoons (1½ inches [4 cm] or 35 g) big. Insert a caramel into the center of each ball of cookie dough and cover with the surrounding dough, re-forming it into a ball. It is important to make sure the bottom of the ball has more dough than the top, as the caramel likes to try to sink to the bottom and create messy cookies when you try to remove them from the pan. I like to slightly flatten the bottom of the cookie dough balls so I remember which end is the bottom.

(continued)

The Best Caramel-Stuffed Brown Butter Pumpkin Cookies (Continued)

Chill the filled dough balls for at least another 30 minutes, then preheat the oven to 350°F (177°C). Note that the cookies do not do well with an overnight chill once the caramel is added because the caramel seeps into the dough too much and will result in a messy baking sheet.

In a bowl, stir together the granulated sugar and cinnamon. Line a rimmed baking sheet with a silicone baking mat.

Quickly roll the filled dough balls in the cinnamon sugar and place at least 2 inches (5 cm) apart on the prepared baking sheet.

Bake for 8 to 10 minutes, or until the edges of the cookies are golden brown and set, but their tops look underdone. Remove from the oven and allow to cool on the baking sheets for at least 3 to 4 minutes before transferring to a wire rack to cool completely.

Store in an airtight container for up to a week at room temperature.

Incredible Gingerbread Cookies with Maple Mascarpone

YIELDS 22 COOKIES

Gingerbread cookies are my favorite holiday cookie from childhood. These are perfectly spiced and the maple mascarpone is a delicious, creamy surprise. You can substitute the mascarpone with full-fat, block-style cream cheese.

FILLING

8 oz (225 g) mascarpone, at room temperature

3 tbsp (63 g) pure maple syrup

3 tbsp (38 g) granulated sugar

1 large egg yolk, at room temperature

¼ tsp ground cinnamon

½ tsp vanilla extract

⅛ tsp sea salt

COOKIE DOUGH

2½ cups (313 g) all-purpose flour

½ tsp sea salt

1 tsp baking soda

1 tbsp (6 g) ground ginger

2 tsp (5 g) ground cinnamon

½ tsp ground cloves

½ tsp ground nutmeg

1 cup (2 sticks/227 g) unsalted butter, at room temperature

1 cup (220 g) light brown sugar

1 large egg, at room temperature

¼ cup (85 g) molasses

½ cup (100 g) granulated sugar, for rolling

1 tsp ground cinnamon, for coating

Make the filling: In the bowl of a stand mixer fitted with the whisk attachment and using medium speed, or in a small bowl with a hand mixer, whisk together the mascarpone, maple syrup, sugar, egg yolk, cinnamon, vanilla and salt together until well mixed. Cover with plastic wrap and chill for at least 2 hours, or until the mixture is somewhat firm.

Make the cookie dough: In a medium-sized bowl, whisk together the flour, salt, baking soda, ginger, cinnamon, cloves and nutmeg, then set aside.

In a separate bowl of your stand mixer fitted with the paddle attachment, beat together the butter and brown sugar on medium speed for 4 to 5 minutes, or until light and fluffy.

Add the egg and molasses to the butter mixture, then beat for another 2 minutes to fully incorporate. Scrape down the sides and bottom of the bowl as needed. Add the flour mixture and mix until just combined and there are no streaks of flour.

In a bowl, combine the granulated sugar and cinnamon.

Portion the dough into balls that are about 2 tablespoons (1¾ inches [4.5 cm] or 45 g) big. Create a large indentation in the top of the dough, add 1½ teaspoons (12 g) of the mascarpone mixture to the indentation, then cover with the surrounding dough. Re-form into a ball, then roll in the cinnamon sugar.

Place the filled dough balls on a parchment paper– or silicone baking mat–lined baking sheet and chill while you preheat the oven.

Preheat the oven to 350°F (177°C) and line another baking sheet for a total of two baking sheets. Divide and separate the cookie dough balls so they are at least 2 inches (5 cm) apart on the two prepared baking sheets.

Bake for 10 to 12 minutes, or until the edges are golden brown. Remove from the oven and allow the cookies to cool on the baking sheets for at least 3 minutes before transferring to a wire rack to cool completely.

Store in an airtight container for up to a week at room temperature.

Sweetheart Red Velvet Sandwiches

YIELDS 10 SANDWICH COOKIES

Red velvet is a nostalgic flavor for me. I love these cookies because they take a classic red velvet cake flavor and make it into a soft, mouthwatering cookie. It's a perfect recipe to have in your repertoire for special occasions.

COOKIE DOUGH

2¼ cups (280 g) all-purpose flour

3 tbsp (15 g) unsweetened cocoa powder

2 tsp (4 g) cornstarch

½ tsp baking powder

½ tsp sea salt

1 cup (200 g) granulated sugar

¼ cup (55 g) light brown sugar

1 cup (2 sticks/227 g) unsalted butter, at room temperature

2 tsp (10 ml) red gel food coloring

1 tsp vanilla extract

1 large egg, at room temperature

FILLING

4 oz (115 g) cream cheese, at room temperature

½ cup (1 stick/114 g) unsalted butter, at room temperature

2 cups (240 g) powdered sugar

⅛ tsp sea salt

1 tsp vanilla extract

1 tbsp (15 ml) heavy cream

Make the cookie dough: In a medium-sized bowl, whisk together the flour, cocoa powder, cornstarch, baking powder and salt, then set aside.

In the bowl of a stand mixer fitted with the whisk attachment, beat together the granulated sugar, brown sugar and butter on medium speed until light and fluffy—this should take 3 to 4 minutes. Scrape down the sides and bottom of the bowl.

Add the food coloring, vanilla and egg to the butter mixture, and beat until fully incorporated, about another 2 minutes. Scrape down the sides and bottom of the bowl as needed.

Gradually add the flour mixture, mixing on low speed, until just incorporated and there are no streaks of flour.

Portion the dough into balls that are about 2 tablespoons (1¾ inches [4.5 cm] or 45 g) big.

Place the dough balls on two parchment-lined rimmed baking sheets and chill for 15 to 20 minutes. While the dough is chilling, preheat the oven to 350°F (177°C).

Separate the dough balls so they are at least 2 inches (5 cm) apart, then bake for 10 to 12 minutes, or until the cookies have spread a bit, are puffy and are just beginning to show signs of light browning on the edges.

Remove from the oven and allow to cool on the baking sheet for 1 minute before transferring to a wire rack to cool completely.

As the cookies cool, make the filling: In the bowl of a stand mixer fitted with the paddle attachment, beat together the cream cheese and butter on medium speed until smooth and creamy, about 3 minutes.

Add the powdered sugar and salt, then beat on medium speed until incorporated, 3 to 4 minutes. Add the vanilla and cream, then beat for another minute.

Turn half of the cookies upside down and spread with the filling. Top with the remaining (right side up) cookies to sandwich them.

Store the cookies in an airtight container at room temperature for up to a week.

Carrot Cake Cookies

YIELDS 20 SANDWICH COOKIES

I've been dreaming of this cookie for years. It's part carrot cake, part cookie, all delicious. This is a great cookie to practice using a fresh ingredient with a higher moisture content and keeping that moisture from turning the cookies into mini cakes.

COOKIE DOUGH

¾ cup (1½ sticks/170 g) unsalted butter

2 cups (250 g) all-purpose flour

1 cup (80 g) old-fashioned rolled oats

1 tbsp (10 g) instant coffee granules

½ tsp baking soda

½ tsp baking powder

1 tsp ground cinnamon

½ tsp ground ginger

¼ tsp ground nutmeg

½ tsp sea salt

¾ cup (165 g) brown sugar

¾ cup (150 g) granulated sugar

2 large eggs, at room temperature

1 tsp vanilla extract

1½ cups (165 g) finely grated carrot

½ cup (40 g) unsweetened shredded coconut

1 cup (110 g) chopped pecans or walnuts

FROSTING

½ cup (1 stick/114 g) unsalted butter, at room temperature

4 oz (115 g) cream cheese, at room temperature

3 cups (360 g) powdered sugar

1 tsp vanilla extract

½ tsp sea salt

1 to 2 tbsp (15 to 30 ml) heavy cream, optional

In a small saucepan, heat the butter over medium heat, stirring frequently, until it smells nutty and has browned in color. Remove from the heat, let cool slightly, then set aside in the refrigerator until halfway solidified.

In a medium-sized bowl, whisk together the flour, oats, instant coffee, baking soda, baking powder, cinnamon, ginger, nutmeg and salt, then set aside.

In the bowl of a stand mixer fitted with the paddle attachment, beat together the butter, brown sugar and granulated sugar on medium speed for 4 to 5 minutes, or until light and fluffy.

Add the eggs and vanilla to the butter mixture, and beat well for another 2 to 3 minutes, or until well incorporated. Scrape down the sides and bottom of the bowl as needed. Add the oat mixture and mix just until there are no streaks of flour.

Pat down the grated carrot with a paper towel to soak up excess moisture. Using a spatula, fold the grated carrot into the batter along with the coconut and chopped nuts until well distributed.

Cover with plastic wrap and chill for at least an hour. Preheat the oven to 350°F (177°C). Line two baking sheets with parchment paper or silicone baking mats.

Portion the dough into balls that are 1 tablespoon (1½ inches [4 cm] or 40 g) big and place 1½ inches (4 cm) apart on the prepared baking sheets. Bake for 8 to 10 minutes, or until the edges are golden brown.

Remove from the oven and allow to cool on the baking sheets for at least 2 minutes before transferring to a wire rack to cool completely.

As the cookies cool, make the frosting: In the bowl of a stand mixer fitted with the paddle attachment, beat together the butter and cream cheese until smooth, 2 to 3 minutes.

Add the powdered sugar, vanilla and salt. Beat until well combined. If the mixture looks lumpy, add the cream, 1 tablespoon (15 ml) at a time, until the frosting is smooth.

Turn half of the cookies upside down and spread with a dollop of the frosting, then top with the remaining (right side up) cookies.

Store in an airtight container for up to a week at room temperature.

Schooltime Peanut Butter and Jelly Linzers

YIELDS 26 SANDWICH COOKIES

Linzer cookies—a buttery, jam-filled sandwich cookie inspired by the Viennese Linzertorte traditionally made with almonds—are a lot of fun to make. This is a great way to learn how to pay close attention to the process of cookie making because you need to make sure you have an equal amount of regular cookies and cookies with the decorative hole. You also need to be careful about how thickly you spread the jam onto the cookies. You may need less than you think!

½ cup (75 g) roasted peanuts

3 cups (375 g) all-purpose flour

½ tsp sea salt

½ tsp baking powder

1 cup (2 sticks/227 g) unsalted butter, at room temperature

½ cup (100 g) granulated sugar

½ cup (110 g) light brown sugar

½ cup (127 g) creamy peanut butter

1 large egg, at room temperature

1 tsp vanilla extract

½ cup (160 g) your choice of jam

⅓ cup (40 g) powdered sugar (optional)

In a food processor, pulse the roasted peanuts until they become a fine powder, but not yet the beginning of peanut butter.

In a medium-sized bowl, whisk together the powdered peanuts, flour, salt and baking powder, then set aside.

In the bowl of a stand mixer fitted with the paddle attachment, beat together the butter, granulated sugar and brown sugar on medium speed for 4 to 5 minutes, or until light and fluffy.

Add the peanut butter, egg and vanilla to the butter mixture, and beat on medium speed until well combined, at least 3 to 4 minutes. Scrape down the sides and bottom of the bowl as needed. Add the flour mixture and beat until just incorporated and there are no streaks of flour.

Turn out the dough onto a sheet of plastic wrap and shape into a 16 x 20–inch (40 x 51–cm) rectangle. Cover with the plastic wrap and chill for at least 4 hours, or overnight.

Preheat the oven to 375°F (190°C) and line two baking sheets with parchment paper or silicone baking mats. You will be baking in batches.

Remove the dough from the plastic wrap and place on a lightly floured surface. Roll out until ¼ inch (6 mm) thick. Use a Linzer cookie cutter to cut out an equal number of solid round cutouts and round cutouts with an opening in the middle—ideally 13 of each.

Place the cutouts at least 1 inch (2.5 cm) apart on the prepared baking sheets and bake for 12 to 13 minutes, or until the edges are golden brown.

Remove from the oven and let cool on the baking sheets for 2 minutes before transferring to a wire rack to cool completely.

Spread a thin layer of the jam on the cooled regular cookies, then top with the cookies with the holes in the center. Sprinkle with powdered sugar, if desired.

Store in an airtight container for up to a week at room temperature.

Pumpkin Chai Snickerdoodle Sandwiches

YIELDS 12 SANDWICHES

I love autumn and all the flavors that become popular during that time. In this recipe, we'll adjust a traditional snickerdoodle to account for the moisture of the pumpkin puree by omitting the egg and using the pumpkin as a binder instead.

PUMPKIN SNICKERDOODLES

2 cups (250 g) all-purpose flour

½ tsp baking soda

½ tsp cream of tartar

¼ tsp baking powder

2 tsp (7 g) pumpkin pie spice

½ tsp sea salt

½ cup (1 stick/114 g) unsalted butter, at room temperature

1 cup (110 g) brown sugar

1 large egg, at room temperature

½ cup (123 g) pure pumpkin puree

2 tsp (10 ml) vanilla extract

¼ cup (50 g) granulated sugar, for rolling

2 tbsp (15 g) ground cinnamon, for rolling

CHAI BUTTERCREAM

½ cup (1 stick/114 g) unsalted butter, at room temperature

1½ cups (180 g) powdered sugar

1 tsp ground cinnamon

1 tsp ground cardamom

½ tsp ground nutmeg

¼ tsp ground cloves

⅛ tsp freshly ground black pepper

1 tsp vanilla extract

1 tbsp (15 ml) heavy cream

In a medium-sized bowl, whisk together the flour, baking soda, cream of tartar, baking powder, pumpkin pie spice and salt, then set aside.

In the bowl of a stand mixer fitted with the paddle attachment, beat together the butter and brown sugar on medium speed until light and fluffy, 4 to 5 minutes.

Add the egg, pumpkin puree and vanilla to the butter mixture. Beat on medium speed until well combined, another 2 to 3 minutes.

Add the flour mixture and mix until just incorporated.

Cover the dough with plastic wrap and refrigerate for 30 minutes.

Preheat the oven to 350°F (177°C) and line two baking sheets with parchment paper or silicone baking mats.

In a small bowl, stir together the granulated sugar and cinnamon.

Portion the dough into balls 1½ tablespoons (1½ inches [4 cm] or 35 g) big and roll in the cinnamon sugar. Place the coated balls at least 2 inches (5 cm) apart on the prepared baking sheets.

Bake for 8 to 10 minutes, or until the edges are a light golden brown. Remove from the oven and let cool on the baking sheets for 2 minutes before transferring to a wire rack to cool completely.

Make the buttercream: In the bowl of a stand mixer fitted with the paddle attachment, beat the butter on medium speed until smooth. Add the powdered sugar. Beat for 3 minutes, scraping down the bowl occasionally, until fully incorporated. Add the cinnamon, cardamom, nutmeg, cloves, pepper and vanilla, and beat to combine. Add the cream and mix well.

Turn half of the cookies upside down and spread the frosting over their upturned bottom, then top with the remaining (right side up) cookies.

Store in an airtight container at room temperature for up to 4 days.

*See photo on page 90.

Apple Pie Cookies

YIELDS 12 SANDWICH COOKIES

I love these cookies because you really learn how to build up layers of flavors by putting together a number of flavors and textures. Not only are we making our own caramel sauce, but we are making a quick homemade apple pie filling and a tasty frosting. If you want to get really creative with the texture, you can add crushed graham crackers or bits of toffee for a nice crunch.

SPECIAL EQUIPMENT

Pastry brush

16-inch (40-cm) piping bag

Large round tip

APPLE CARAMEL

1½ cups (300 g) granulated sugar

¼ cup (60 ml) water

¾ cup (175 ml) heavy cream, warmed

½ cup (1 stick/114 g) unsalted butter, at room temperature

½ tsp sea salt

3 tbsp (45 g) apple butter, at room temperature

½ tsp vanilla extract

APPLE PIE FILLING

2 cups (240 g) peeled, cored and chopped Granny Smith apples

⅓ cup (73 g) packed brown sugar

2 tbsp (28 g) unsalted butter, at room temperature

½ tsp ground cinnamon

¼ tsp ground ginger

⅛ tsp ground nutmeg

1½ tsp (8 ml) cold water (optional)

1 tbsp (7 g) cornstarch (optional)

Make the caramel: In a large, heavy-bottomed saucepan, combine the sugar and water and heat over medium-high heat. Do not stir. Allow the sugar to cook down until it turns a deep amber color. As the sugar cooks, wet a pastry brush and wipe down the sides of the saucepan to dissolve any stray sugar crystals.

In a microwave-safe bowl, microwave the cream for 30 to 45 seconds, just until it begins to steam. As soon as the caramel is that deep amber color, turn off the heat and carefully pour in the heated cream. Keep your head away from the saucepan as it will bubble up a lot!

Stir the mixture gently until the heavy cream incorporates. If the caramel seizes, heat it over low heat on the stovetop until it loosens again.

Add the butter and salt. Stir until fully combined, then stir in the apple butter and vanilla.

Pour the caramel into a heatproof container and let cool to room temperature. Cover with plastic wrap and set aside. The caramel sauce can be stored in an airtight container in the refrigerator for up to a week in advance. Warm in the microwave when ready to use.

Make the apple pie filling: In a medium-sized skillet, combine the apples, brown sugar, butter, cinnamon, ginger and nutmeg and cook over medium heat until the apples are fork-tender. If you find the juices need to thicken more, in a small bowl, stir together the water and cornstarch, then pour half of the mixture into the apple mixture. Cook until the juices become clear again, and then for a minute longer. If it still isn't thick, add the remaining cornstarch mixture and cook until clear again. Place in a heatproof container to cool to room temperature.

The apple pie filling can be made up to a week in advance, if stored in an airtight container in the refrigerator.

(continued)

Apple Pie Cookies (Continued)

COOKIES

2¼ cups (281 g) all-purpose flour

1 tsp ground cinnamon

½ tsp ground ginger

½ tsp ground cardamom

¼ tsp ground nutmeg

¾ tsp baking soda

½ tsp baking powder

½ tsp sea salt

½ cup (1 stick/114 g) unsalted butter, at room temperature

1¼ cups (250 g) granulated sugar

2 tbsp (30 ml) milk, at room temperature

1 large egg, at room temperature

1 tsp vanilla extract

FROSTING

4 oz (115 g) cream cheese, at room temperature

½ cup (1 stick/114 g) unsalted butter, at room temperature

2 cups (240 g) powdered sugar

½ tsp vanilla extract

½ tsp ground cinnamon

⅛ tsp sea salt

2 tbsp (30 ml) heavy cream, at room temperature

Make the cookies: Preheat the oven to 350°F (177°C) and line two baking sheets with parchment paper or silicone baking mats.

In a medium-sized bowl, whisk together the flour, cinnamon, ginger, cardamom, nutmeg, baking soda, baking powder and salt, then set aside.

In the bowl of a stand mixer fitted with the paddle attachment, beat together the butter and granulated sugar on medium speed for 4 to 5 minutes, or until light and fluffy.

Add the milk, egg and vanilla to the butter mixture. Beat on medium speed for another 3 to 4 minutes. Scrape down the sides and bottom of the bowl as needed.

Beat in the flour mixture until just combined and there are no streaks of flour.

Portion the dough into balls that are about 2 tablespoons (1¾ inches [4.5 cm] or 45 g) big. Flatten them into uniform disks, and place them about 2 inches (5 cm) apart on the prepared baking sheets.

Bake for 6 to 8 minutes, or until the edges become a light golden brown. Remove from the oven and let cool on the baking sheets for at least 5 minutes before transferring to a wire rack to cool completely.

Make the frosting: In the bowl of a stand mixer fitted with the paddle attachment, beat together the cream cheese and butter until smooth and creamy. Add the powdered sugar, vanilla, cinnamon and salt and beat to incorporate. Add the cream, 1 tablespoon (15 ml) at a time, until you get a spreadable consistency.

Fit a piping bag with a round tip and fill with the frosting. Turn over half of the cookies and pipe a ring all around just inside the outer edge of the upturned upside-down cookies, leaving an empty space in the center. Fill each center with a spoonful of the apple pie filling. Drizzle the apple caramel over the frosting and filling, then top with the remaining (right side up) cookies.

Store in an airtight container for up to 3 days in the refrigerator.

Swoon-Worthy Fig and Date Newtons

YIELDS 27 COOKIES

This recipe is great practice for carefully handling filled dough. When cutting the dough, keep a clean kitchen towel dampened with warm water to clean the knife, as the filling can be sticky.

COOKIE DOUGH

½ cup (1 stick/114 g) unsalted butter, at room temperature

½ cup (110 g) brown sugar

1 large egg white, at room temperature

1 tsp vanilla extract

1½ cups (188 g) all-purpose flour, plus more for dusting

¼ tsp baking powder

¼ tsp sea salt

FILLING

8 oz (225 g) dried pitted dates, chopped

8 oz (225 g) dried figs, chopped

½ cup (120 ml) fresh orange juice

¾ cup (175 ml) water

2 tbsp (30 ml) pure maple syrup

1 tsp ground cinnamon

½ tsp sea salt

1 tsp vanilla extract

Make the cookie dough: In the bowl of a stand mixer fitted with the paddle attachment, beat together the butter and brown sugar on medium speed for about 5 minutes, or until light and fluffy. Scrape down the sides and bottom with a rubber spatula. Add the egg white and vanilla and beat on medium speed for about a minute, or until fully combined.

Add the flour, baking powder and salt, then mix on low speed until just incorporated. Place the dough onto a sheet of plastic wrap and form into a 4 x 6–inch (10 x 15–cm) rectangle. Wrap tightly in the plastic wrap and chill for at least an hour.

Make the filling: In a medium-sized saucepan, combine the dates, figs, orange juice, water, maple syrup, cinnamon, salt and vanilla, and heat over medium heat until the mixture comes to a boil. Lower the heat to medium-low, or until it is at a simmer. Continue to cook, stirring occasionally with a wooden spoon, until the mixture is the consistency of jam, 6 to 10 minutes. Remove from the heat and let cool to room temperature. Transfer the mixture to a food processor and pulse until it is a smooth paste.

On a lightly floured surface, roll out the dough to a 12 x 16–inch (30 x 41–cm) rectangle. Cut the dough down its length so you have three 4-inch (10-cm)-wide strips.

Spread a thick 1-inch (2.5-cm)-wide layer of the fig puree down the center of each strip. Fold the left side of the dough over the strip of puree, then fold the right side over that. You may need to chill the dough during this process if the dough feels too soft to handle.

Flip the dough over so the seams from the folding are facing down, then place the filled strips on a parchment-lined baking sheet to chill.

Preheat the oven to 350°F (177°C). Line two baking sheets with parchment paper or silicone baking mats.

Remove the filled strips from the refrigerator and use a sharp knife to cut them into 1½-inch (4-cm) pieces. Have a towel and bowl of water ready to wash the knife if it becomes too sticky.

Place the filled Newtons 1 inch (2.5 cm) apart on your prepared baking sheets and bake for 15 minutes, or until light brown. Remove from the oven and let cool. The cookies are better the next day, after the dough has time to soften.

Store in an airtight container in the refrigerator for up to 2 weeks.

Senior Cookies

Advanced and Technical Cookies

These are my favorite kind of cookies. They're always exciting and really stretch your skills during your baking journey. Once you master these, you reach a level of confidence and satisfaction with cookies that is hard to beat. You'll learn why accuracy is so important and why timing and even the weather outside matters. Most of these cookies will take time to get perfect, but they're fun and delicious enough to keep you motivated to keep baking.

Get excited, because there are so many tiny yet massively important techniques here. We will start off easier with tuile recipes, which require batter control, careful timing and patience. We then blend the need for precision and speed/timing with fortune cookies and stroopwafels.

Everything we do in this chapter, and what we've been working on in previous chapters, culminates to finally tackling and hopefully mastering two methods for making macarons, which are considered some of the most difficult and finicky cookies to make. Even professional bakers who make hundreds of macarons a day still get the occasional bad batch, so don't feel bad if your first few attempts aren't perfect. As long as you follow the directions, they'll still taste amazing regardless of how they look!

Chocolate Tuile Cigars

YIELDS 16 COOKIES

Tuiles are a French cookie (the word translates to "tile") and are known for being wafer-thin, delicate cookies that are perfect for molding into different shapes while they're still warm. I love these chocolate tuile cigars because they make a delicious garnish for ice cream or panna cotta, or are delicious on their own when filled with whipped cream.

¼ cup (½ stick/57 g) unsalted butter, at room temperature

⅓ cup (40 g) powdered sugar

½ cup (63 g) all-purpose flour

1½ tbsp (8 g) Dutch-processed cocoa powder

2 large egg whites, at room temperature

4 oz (115 g) semisweet chocolate

2 tbsp (40 g) finely crushed nuts of your choice

Preheat the oven to 475°F (246°C). Line two rimmed baking sheets with parchment paper or silicone baking mats.

In the bowl of a stand mixer fitted with the paddle attachment, beat together the butter and powdered sugar on medium speed until light and fluffy, about 3 minutes.

Add the flour and cocoa powder, then mix until just combined.

Add the egg whites and beat until the mixture is completely smooth—this can take 3 to 4 minutes.

Spread a tablespoon (15 ml) of the batter onto one half of one prepared baking sheet and spread it into a 5-inch (13-cm) circle. Repeat on the other half of the pan. You will bake the tuiles in batches of one pan at a time.

Bake for 2 to 3 minutes, or until the edges look set. Remove the cookies from the oven and use an offset spatula to loosen them from the baking sheet, then roll them into tubes. You can wrap the cookies around the handle of a wooden spoon to help. Continue to bake the next two cookies while the previous batch cools, until all 16 cookies are baked and rolled up.

In a small, microwave-safe bowl, microwave the chocolate for 30 seconds. Remove the chocolate from the microwave and stir well, and repeat as needed until it is fully melted. Place the crushed nuts in another small bowl. Dip one end of each cookie into the chocolate, then into the nuts.

Store in an airtight container for up to a week at room temperature.

Make-Your-Own Fortune Cookies

YIELDS 14 TO 16 COOKIES

You usually get fortune cookies in Chinese restaurants, but they were actually invented by Japanese American immigrants, based on a cookie from Japan. I think they're a lot better made at home. To make it easier to source, we are basing our recipe on a classic tuile cookie. It is important to make the cookies in batches of two and to work swiftly. Before you start baking, get your fortunes ready: Cut paper into 2¼ x ½–inch (5.5 x 1.3–cm) strips and write whatever fortunes you want on them.

SPECIAL EQUIPMENT

Kitchen gloves

Muffin tin

4 large egg whites, at room temperature

¾ cup (150 g) granulated sugar

1 cup (125 g) all-purpose flour

¼ tsp salt

5 tbsp (71 g) unsalted butter, melted

3 tbsp (45 ml) heavy cream, at room temperature

1 tsp vanilla extract

Preheat the oven to 400°F (205°C). Line a baking sheet with a silicone baking mat—not parchment paper.

In the bowl of a stand mixer fitted with the paddle attachment, beat together the egg whites and sugar on medium speed for 1 minute to ensure they are well combined.

Add the flour, salt, butter, cream and vanilla. Beat just until the mixture is smooth.

Pour a couple of tablespoons (about 30 ml) of the batter onto one half of the prepared baking sheet and spread it out until it is a circle about 5 inches (13 cm) in diameter. Do not worry about having perfectly round circles. Repeat to fit another round on the baking sheet for a total of two circles.

Bake for 5 to 7 minutes, or until the edges of the cookies are a warm golden brown.

Work quickly! Remove from the oven and run an offset spatula under the cookies.

Add a fortune slip to the middle of each cookie. Fold each cookie in half to form a semicircle, and then fold to point the two ends of your semicircle together to make the shape of a fortune cookie. You can use the rim of a cup to help make that shape. You must shape the cookies while they're still fresh from the oven, so you might want to wear kitchen gloves to protect your fingers.

Place each fortune cookie in the well of a muffin tin to hold its shape as it cools.

Repeat with the remaining batter, making only two cookies at a time, until you have used up all your batter. Once all of your cookies have cooled, enjoy your custom fortune cookies!

Store in an airtight container for up to a week at room temperature.

Totally Orange Almond Lace Cookies

YIELDS 30 COOKIES

Lace cookies are just as delicate as tuiles, possibly even more so. They're an interesting cookie to learn how to make because the dough must be warm and batterlike in consistency for them to bake correctly. In fact, if you find your batter starts to thicken too much, you can and should thin it again with a teaspoon or two of orange juice.

¼ cup (½ stick/57 g) unsalted butter

2 tbsp (30 ml) heavy cream

1 tbsp (15 ml) orange juice, plus more as needed

1 tsp orange zest

¾ cup (75 g) almond flour

1 tbsp (8 g) all-purpose flour

½ cup (100 g) sugar

Preheat the oven to 375°F (191°C) and line two rimmed baking sheets with parchment paper or silicone baking mats.

In a small saucepan, combine the butter, cream and orange juice and heat over medium heat until the butter is melted but the mixture is not bubbling.

Add the zest, almond flour, flour and sugar to the saucepan and mix well. Cook just until the mixture begins to bubble—this can take up to 3 minutes. Remove from the heat, but keep warm.

Place five rounds that are each about ½ teaspoon big at equal distances from one another on the prepared baking sheets. Each ½ teaspoon should be spread out to a thin layer about 2½ inches (7 cm) wide.

You will need to bake these in batches of one sheet at a time. Reheat the batter, as needed, if it starts to cool too much; it needs to stay fairly liquid.

Bake one pan for 6 to 7 minutes, or until the cookies are lightly browned. Remove from the oven and bake your next batch, leaving the baked cookies on their baking sheet for about 1 minute before transferring to a parchment-lined wire rack to cool completely.

Store in an airtight container for up to 3 days at room temperature. Place parchment paper between each layer of the cookies to prevent potential sticking.

Mouthwatering Stroopwafels

YIELDS 28 TO 30 COOKIES

I am obsessed with stroopwafels. If you are new to them, they are a delicious Dutch treat made with a thin yeasted waffle cookie that is split in half and filled with caramel. You need to work quickly to cut the waffles before they harden, so this is a great test on your efficiency and timing. Wait until all your waffle cookies are cut before adding the caramel, which will soften them back up. My caramel is a little different from what you'd typically find in these cookies because it is actually a little lighter and more delicate in flavor, with a delicious hint of cinnamon.

SPECIAL EQUIPMENT

Pastry brush

Waffle cone iron

Kitchen gloves

CARAMEL

2 cups (400 g) granulated sugar

¼ cup (60 ml) water

⅔ cup (160 ml) heavy cream, warmed

2 tbsp (28 g) unsalted butter, at room temperature

2 tsp (10 ml) vanilla extract

½ tsp ground cinnamon

¾ tsp sea salt

Make the caramel: In a large, heavy-bottomed saucepan, heat the sugar and water together over medium-high heat and let cook undisturbed until the mixture reaches a deep amber color. This can take anywhere between 15 and 20 minutes. It is important to keep an eye on the color of the caramel so it doesn't get too dark. If the color becomes too dark, the caramel will taste burnt and bitter. While the sugar cooks down and caramelizes, you should use a pastry brush dipped in water to wipe down any sugar crystals from the side of the saucepan. Turn off the heat.

While the caramel is cooking, in a small, microwave-safe bowl, microwave the cream until it is steamy and hot to the touch—this should take 30 to 45 seconds.

Slowly add the warmed cream to the fully caramelized mixture—it will bubble a lot, so beware! If the caramel starts to seize (you'll know this is happening if the caramel starts to harden once you add the cream), you can stir the mixture and it should start to loosen. If after a couple of minutes of stirring the mixture doesn't loosen, you can turn the heat to low beneath the saucepan to help.

Add the butter and vanilla, and stir well. Add the cinnamon and salt, and mix well. Allow to cool completely to room temperature. The caramel may be made days or even weeks in advance. Pour it into a container and cover with plastic wrap, then store in the refrigerator until needed.

(continued)

COOKIES

½ cup (120 ml) warm milk (110 to 120°F [43 to 49°C])

2¼ tsp (9 g) active dry yeast

¾ cup (150 g) granulated sugar, divided

4 cups (500 g) all-purpose flour

1 tsp ground cinnamon

½ tsp sea salt

1 cup (2 sticks/227 g) unsalted butter, cubed, at room temperature

2 large eggs, lightly beaten, at room temperature

Neutral oil, for waffle cone iron (optional)

Extra Credit: *If you want to deepen the flavors of the cookie and/or the caramel, you can replace the granulated sugar with brown sugar. You can also add other warm spices, such as ginger and cardamom, to the cookie or caramel using the same amounts as you do the cinnamon.*

Make the waffle cookies: Place the warm milk in a small bowl and whisk in the yeast. Add a teaspoon of the sugar to the mixture. Allow the mixture to sit until the top has a thick layer of foam, about 5 minutes. If there is no foam, then the yeast is dead and you need to start over with fresh yeast.

In the bowl of a stand mixer fitted with the whisk attachment, whisk together the flour, remaining sugar, cinnamon and salt on low speed until combined.

Add the butter, one cube at a time, and mix until the mixture resembles bread crumbs.

Add the eggs and the yeast mixture, and mix to combine. Continue to mix until the dough comes together and is only a little sticky to the touch. Normally, when using yeast, you want to knead the mixture to develop the gluten; however, this is not necessary with these cookies. We want everything to be just combined. Do not be tempted to knead the dough. Cover the dough with plastic wrap.

Set aside to rest for 45 minutes in a warm, dry area. The dough will not rise very much during this time.

Warm the caramel if it feels too thick to spread. You can do this by heating it in a microwave for 25 to 45 seconds and stirring well.

Preheat a waffle cone iron on the medium-high setting. Lightly brush with oil if your iron is not nonstick. Form the dough into equal-sized balls, about 2 tablespoons (35 g) each, and place one in the waffle cone iron.

Shut the iron lid and press down lightly, but don't clamp closed. Bake until crisp and golden, 1 to 2 minutes.

Quickly transfer the waffle cookie onto a flat surface. While it is still hot, using a sharp knife, swiftly but carefully cut the waffle in half along its side, then use a round cutter that is 3½ inches (9 cm) in diameter to cut out a disk from each waffle half. Cutting the waffle cookie as it cools is difficult and nearly impossible, thus the need for speed. Use kitchen gloves to protect your fingers from burning. (No burnt fingers here, please!)

Dollop a hefty 1 to 1½ teaspoons (15 to 20 ml) of the caramel onto one waffle disk and spread until it almost reaches the edges, then top with the second waffle disk. Set aside to cool.

Store in an airtight container for up to a week at room temperature.

Autumn-Spiced Palmiers

YIELDS 30 COOKIES

Palmiers go by many different nicknames; it would be hard to name them all. They're a flaky, buttery treat that is usually filled with sugar, and sometimes spices. You can also add other things, such as citrus zest and finely chopped dried fruits. The basis of the cookie is puff pastry, which is what gives you those irresistible flakes. It is easier than you might think to make this at home. All you need is patience (it takes a while to make), and a love for butter. You will get the best results using a tapered wooden rolling pin, but technically, you can use any rolling pin you have available.

COOKIE DOUGH

2 cups (250 g) all-purpose flour

1 tsp sea salt

3 tbsp (43 g) unsalted butter, at room temperature

½ cup (120 ml) cold water

½ cup (60 g) powdered sugar, for rolling

½ cup (100 g) granulated sugar, for rolling

BUTTER PACKET

2 tbsp (15 g) all-purpose flour, divided

1 cup (2 sticks/227 g) unsalted butter, at almost room temperature

Make the cookie dough: On a clean surface, combine the flour and salt in a mound, then create a well in the middle of the mound.

Add the butter to the well, then slowly mix the butter into the flour—fingers, fork, pastry cutter all work. Slowly add the water as you mix in the butter and continue to work the mixture until it comes together into a dough.

Shape the dough into an 8-inch (20-cm) square, then transfer to a sheet of plastic wrap. Wrap tightly in the plastic wrap and chill for at least 30 minutes.

Make the butter packet: Lightly flour a sheet of parchment paper and add the butter. Top with another light sprinkling of flour before topping with another sheet of parchment paper.

Use a rolling pin to beat the butter until it flattens, there are no lumps and it all comes together. You may need to lift the top sheet of parchment paper to readjust the butter to encourage it to come together properly. Add another sprinkling of flour, if needed, to help make the butter easier to handle and come together better. You might not need all the flour.

Form the butter into a square that is roughly 1 inch (2.5 cm) smaller on every side than the dough square. Wrap in plastic wrap and refrigerate for 25 minutes.

Dust your surface and rolling pin with powdered sugar and place the dough square on the prepared surface. Roll out the square to an 8 x 12–inch (20 x 30–cm) rectangle, taking care that the 8-inch (20-cm) width of the rectangle doesn't get any wider.

Remove the butter from its plastic wrap and place in the center of the rectangle, then fold the top and then the bottom of the 12-inch (30-cm) length of the rectangle over the butter square, like folding a letter. Use your fingers to ensure the edges are sealed.

(continued)

Autumn-Spiced Palmiers (Continued)

FILLING

3 tbsp (43 g) unsalted butter, melted

1 tsp orange zest

⅓ cup (67 g) granulated sugar

1 tsp ground cinnamon

½ tsp ground ginger

⅛ tsp sea salt

Dust the surface with more powdered sugar as needed, then turn the dough 90 degrees. Again roll out the dough into an 8 x 12–inch (20 x 30–cm) rectangle, and fold the top and bottom of the 12-inch (30-cm) length of the rectangle over the center of the dough. Cover with plastic wrap and chill for 1 hour.

Unwrap the dough again and, on the surface again dusted with powdered sugar, roll out into another rectangle with the same dimensions as before. Fold the top and then the bottom over the center. Turn again by 90 degrees, then roll into a rectangle as earlier, before again folding the top and bottom over the center. Wrap in plastic wrap and chill for at least 30 minutes.

Now dust your surface with granulated sugar. Unwrap the dough and divide it in half. Roll each half into a rectangle 4 to 5 inches (10 to 13 cm) wide and ¼ inch (6 mm) thick.

Brush the rectangles with melted butter. In a small bowl, stir together the zest, sugar, cinnamon, ginger and salt, then sprinkle evenly over the melted butter.

Fold the ends of each rectangle lengthwise so they meet in the center, then fold them in half again so the first folds are sandwiched in the middle. Place on a rimmed baking sheet and chill for about 25 minutes, for easier cutting.

Preheat the oven to 400°F (204°C) and line two baking sheets with parchment paper.

Cut the folded dough into pieces about ½ inch (1.3 cm) thick, then set them, cut side down, 1 to 2 inches (2.5 to 5 cm) apart on the prepared baking sheets.

Bake for 10 to 12 minutes, or until they are puffed and golden brown. Remove from the oven and allow to cool on the baking sheets for 3 to 5 minutes before transferring to a wire rack.

Store in an airtight container for up to a week at room temperature.

Light-as-a-Cloud Meringue Cookies

Whenever I move to a new place, my first baked good is always a meringue cookie. It's always been tradition to check for hot spots in the oven and make sure the internal temperature is correct (see page 11 for more on this), since these are so important for meringue cookies. Meringue cookies should be light and airy with a delightful crunch. They make great decorations on other baked treats but are also incredible just as they are, infused with flavor. However, they can be finicky. You don't want to make them during a humid day, as that can stop them from drying out properly. You must also make sure everything that touches the egg whites is thoroughly cleaned of any traces of fat, otherwise the meringue may collapse. My best tip is to rub everything down with something acidic, such as vinegar or a lemon slice. Meringues also require a lot of patience because they take hours before they're ready to eat.

Fruit-Swirled Meringue Cookies

YIELDS ABOUT 30 COOKIES

Meringue cookies are a delightful treat, especially when swirled with jam. The swirls of fruit gives the meringue a sweet, bright pop of flavor. For the best results, fold in the jam very gently without mixing it in too much, otherwise you might end up with a collapsed meringue that is still tasty, but not easy to handle.

---

3 large egg whites (105 g), at room temperature

¼ tsp cream of tartar

½ tsp sea salt

¾ cup (150 g) granulated sugar

½ tsp vanilla extract

⅓ cup (107 g) jam of your choice

Wash and dry the bowl of your stand mixer and its whisk attachment thoroughly, then lightly rub them down with something acidic, such as vinegar or lemon. Set aside. This is to ensure that there are no traces of fat on your equipment that can stop the meringue from forming.

Preheat your oven to 250°F (121°C) and line one rimmed baking sheet with parchment paper.

In the bowl of a stand mixer fitted with the paddle attachment, beat together the egg whites, cream of tartar and salt on medium speed until the mixture is very foamy.

Start adding the sugar, ¼ cup (50 g) at a time, while mixing, waiting at least 30 seconds between each addition. Add the vanilla.

Increase the speed to medium-high and continue to whip the egg whites until the mixture looks glossy and stiff peaks form. To check for stiff peaks, stop the mixer and remove the whisk attachment. Dip the whisk into the meringue and hold it upward. If the end of the meringue droops over, the meringue is not ready. If the meringue sticks up, it has reached stiff peaks.

(continued)

Fruit-Swirled Meringue Cookies
(Continued)

Add the jam, 2 to 3 tablespoons (42 to 63 g) at a time, very gently folding it in using a rubber spatula, making sure to keep nice swirls in the meringue.

Use a large spoon to drop a large spoonful of the meringue onto your prepared baking sheet and gently swirl into a cookielike shape—I typically make them about 3 inches (8 cm) wide. Alternatively, you can fill a piping bag fitted with your favorite tip and pipe shapes with your meringue about 1 inch (2.5 cm) apart onto your prepared baking sheet.

Bake for about 45 minutes, or until the outside of the meringue feels crisp to the touch. It may take longer if the humidity is over 60 percent outside. Do not open the oven door to peek at the meringue cookies until they are near the end of the baking time. Turn off the oven and leave the meringues in the oven with the door closed for at least an hour.

Remove from the oven and allow them to cool completely.

Store in an airtight container for up to a week at room temperature.

Extra Credit: *You can omit the jam or use any number of extracts. Spices, such as cinnamon and ginger, are also great. Lemon and orange zest also add a lovely brightness to the meringue.*

Strawberry-Covered Chocolate Kisses

YIELDS ABOUT 30 COOKIES

I love these meringue kisses because they are so much fun to make and the chocolate surprise is such a delight. It's a fun challenge to use freeze-dried strawberries to give the meringues a natural strawberry flavor without impacting the delicate meringue too much. This is great for working on your piping skills, too!

SPECIAL EQUIPMENT

16-inch (40-cm) piping bag

Piping tip

1 cup (30 g) freeze-dried strawberries, divided

3 large egg whites (105 g), at room temperature

¼ tsp cream of tartar

½ tsp sea salt

¾ cup (150 g) granulated sugar

½ tsp vanilla extract

30 chocolate kisses

Line two rimmed baking sheets with parchment paper or silicone baking mats. Set aside. Preheat the oven to 250°F (121°C).

In a food processor, process the freeze-dried strawberries until they become a fine powder. Set aside.

Wash and dry the bowl of your stand mixer and the whisk attachment. Rub them down with something acidic, such as vinegar or lemon. This is to ensure that there are no traces of fat on your equipment that can stop the meringue from forming.

Add the egg whites to the bowl and beat on medium speed until the mixture is almost doubled in size.

Add the cream of tartar, salt, sugar, three-quarters of the ground freeze-dried strawberries and the vanilla, then increase the speed to medium-high.

Beat until the mixture is glossy and reaches stiff peaks.

Fit a 16-inch (40-cm) piping bag with your favorite piping tip and fill two-thirds of the way with the meringue.

Pipe a small dollop of the meringue onto a prepared baking sheet, then top it with a chocolate kiss, pressing gently only to make sure it is held in place but does not touch the bottom. Pipe the meringue over the kiss until it is completely covered. Repeat with the remaining meringue and kisses until you have 15 mounds on each prepared pan, spacing 1 inch (2.5 cm) apart. Dust all of them lightly with the remaining freeze-dried strawberries.

Bake for 40 to 45 minutes, or until the meringue is dried and crisp to the touch. Turn off the oven and leave the meringues in the oven with the door closed for at least an hour, then remove.

Store in an airtight container for up to a week at room temperature.

*See photo on page 124.

Mastering Macarons

Macarons are considered one of the most difficult cookies to make. Even master bakers deal with temperamental macarons that have hollows or cracks. There are two main methods I like to use for making macarons, and I'll cover both in this section. French macarons are the trickiest to bake, but that is partially why they are most coveted. I like Swiss macarons because they are more forgiving and you're more likely to get consistent results every time.

Try French macarons if you are confident in your meringue-making skills, have an eye for detail and precision . . . and enjoy a challenge. Bonus points if you are more concerned about perfecting your skill than getting perfect macarons every time you make them.

Go for Swiss macarons if you are less confident in the kitchen, want something more forgiving and aren't sure if you can get your *macaronage* just right. They are also great if you need consistently good results every time you are baking and don't mind a bit of an arm workout.

For the best results, I recommend reading through the directions a few times before you start anything. I also recommend reading through "Macaron Troubleshooting" (page 159), as it provides plenty of information for you to check through before you begin and will give you the greatest chance of success and of understanding how to improve your macarons should they not come out well. You should also make these on days with lower humidity. High humidity can prevent the macarons from forming the dried-out top we need prior to baking.

We will test out your patience and accuracy and come out victorious! It is important to not try to cut corners here. Yes, you do need a kitchen scale for the shells. No, you cannot convert the grams to volume and hope for the best. Trust me, I've tried.

Make sure to give yourself ample time to make them. Unlike working with most cookies, you really need to be patient and wait for exactly when the macarons tell you that they are ready at each stage.

The most important thing to know is that your first batch probably won't come out looking perfect. Your second batch might not, either, but your macarons will keep looking better the more you make them. No matter how they look, they will still taste amazing, and that is all that truly matters! (Hey, worse comes to worst, they make a great addition to a thick and creamy milk shake, or mixed into your favorite ice cream!)

When you are comfortable making the macarons you find in the book, you can get adventurous with flavor pairings and even substituting the almond flour with other types of nut flours.

KEY TERMS

Before you begin baking, I want to share some key terms that you will need to know. You will see these terms while reading the instructions, and they will become important when troubleshooting any potential issues with your macarons.

Shells: Shells are the finished product that we mix, pipe and bake. They are the technical aspect of the macarons we fill with frosting, pastry cream, jam and more.

Feet: Around the bottom of the macaron shells, you will find a textured ring. These are called the feet.

Hollows: Hollow macaron shells are ones that seem nice on the outside, but upon opening one, you find there is an air pocket at the top of the shell.

Folding: This is the technique of gently mixing the almond flour mixture into the meringue to create your batter. It is achieved by scooping your spatula under everything at the bottom of the bowl and bringing it up to fold on top of everything that is at the top of the bowl.

Macaronage: This is the stage in which your batter is ready to be piped. The meringue is deflated and the almond flour mixture is combined just enough that the batter flows similarly to lava.

Maturing: This is aging the finished macarons to further develop the flavors so they are more intense and enjoyable. It also helps improve the final texture of the macarons.

French Macarons

As I mentioned earlier, French macarons are some of the trickiest macarons to make. This is because French meringue is more delicate than Swiss or Italian meringue. But the tradeoff is worth it, because you get a more delicious and therefore more delectable cookie. As with the meringue cookies, we need to keep our equipment free from any traces of fat. French macarons also work best with aged egg whites because aging helps remove some of the excess moisture, which will get you a better final meringue. This means you can't make French macarons on a whim. Instead, you need to prep the day before by leaving your egg whites out overnight.

Boston Cream Pie Macarons

YIELDS ABOUT 18 SANDWICH COOKIES

Boston cream pie donuts were my absolute favorite growing up. I love them in macaron form, too. It is hard to stop at just one or two . . . or even five of these! The recipe does give you extra filling, but you can find many ways to eat up the rest (like with a spoon by the fridge!)

EQUIPMENT

Kitchen scale

2 medium-sized bowls

Balloon whisk

2-quart (2-L) saucepan

Fine-mesh strainer

Plastic wrap

Food processor

Sifter (optional)

Stand mixer with whisk attachment

Silicone spatula

3 rimmed baking sheets

Parchment paper or silicone baking mats

2 (16-inch [40-cm]) piping bags

2 round piping tips

Toothpick

Microwave-safe bowl

FILLING

3 large (60 g) egg yolks

5 tbsp (65 g) granulated sugar

1½ tbsp (15 g) cornstarch

1½ tbsp (15 g) all-purpose flour

1¼ cups (395 ml) whole milk

2 tsp (10 ml) vanilla extract

Make the pastry cream filling: In a medium-sized bowl, whisk together the egg yolks and granulated sugar until pale yellow and creamy, then whisk in the cornstarch and flour. Set aside.

In a 2-quart (2-L) saucepan, heat the milk over medium heat until it is simmering and bubbling at the rim. Remove from the heat.

Pour the hot milk into the egg mixture in a slow drizzle while simultaneously whisking constantly until the mixture is smooth.

Transfer the mixture back to the saucepan. Cook over medium-low heat, whisking constantly and vigorously so that the eggs won't curdle, until the mixture visibly thickens.

(continued)

Boston Cream Pie Macarons (Continued)

SHELLS

200 g powdered sugar

100 g almond flour

Lemon wedge, for cleaning equipment

120 g egg whites (from about 4 large eggs), left out overnight

¼ tsp salt

40 g granulated sugar

1 to 2 drops gel food coloring in color of your choice (optional, but recommended)

1 to 2 tsp (5 to 10 ml) vanilla extract

Strain the pastry cream into a separate medium-sized bowl, using a fine-mesh strainer, and press plastic wrap to directly touch the surface of the cream. This is to prevent it from developing a skin.

Let cool to room temperature, then chill until ready to assemble the macarons. It may be made up to a day in advance.

Make the macaron shells: In a food processor, combine the powdered sugar and almond flour and pulse 10 to 15 times. Pour the mixture through a fine-mesh strainer or sifter. For the best results, you should sift the mixture a second time. Set aside.

Wash and dry your stand mixer bowl and its whisk attachment. Gently rub with a slice of lemon and wipe dry again. This is to make sure there are no traces of fat on your equipment, which would prevent the egg whites from rising into a meringue.

Add the egg whites and salt. Beat the egg whites on medium speed until foamy, then slowly increase the speed to medium-high. Add the granulated sugar and beat until the mixture looks glossy and reaches stiff peaks. You can check whether the meringue has stiff peaks by removing the whisk from the mixer and dipping it into the meringue. Flip the whisk upside down: If the meringue points up, it is stiff; if it droops, it needs more mixing.

Mix in the food coloring and vanilla. Add the almond flour mixture and use a silicone spatula to mix it into the meringue. Spread the mixture along the sides of the mixer bowl, then scrape it down and gently stir. You want to deflate the meringue and remove as much air as possible. Do this motion until your mixture moves around like lava. Test this by occasionally lifting up some of the batter and letting it drop down back into the bowl. It should drip down like a ribbon and then slowly incorporate back into the batter. If it just sits there or falls in clumps, mix longer.

Set aside for 30 minutes to allow any remaining air to leave the batter. Line three rimmed baking sheets with parchment paper or silicone baking mats.

Fit a round piping tip into a 16-inch (40-cm) piping bag and fill the bag halfway with the batter. Pipe rounds that are 1 to 1½ inches (2.5 to 4 cm) wide and about 1 inch (2.5 cm) apart onto the prepared baking sheets. Refill the bag as needed, but always make sure it is never more than halfway filled.

GANACHE

½ cup (120 ml) heavy cream

4 oz (115 g) semisweet chocolate

Tap the baking sheets against your counter to help release any remaining air bubbles. Use a toothpick to pop any air bubbles that you see rise up. If there are any points from the piping, you can use a wet finger to press it down so the tops are flat.

Leave the sheets alone for at least 45 minutes to an hour, or until the tops are dry enough to touch without the batter sticking to your fingers. This is important to ensure the macarons have smooth tops and develop proper feet.

Preheat the oven to 325°F (163°C) and bake the macarons, one sheet at a time, for 10 minutes, turning the sheet halfway through. Check that the macarons are ready to be removed by testing whether a macaron can be lifted off the baking sheet without breaking. Check every minute if the macarons are not ready after the first 10 minutes.

Remove from the oven and leave the macarons on the baking sheet for 5 minutes before transferring to a wire rack to cool completely. Bake the remaining macarons, one sheet at a time, and let cool completely.

Make the ganache: In a microwave-safe bowl, microwave the cream for between 1 and 2 minutes, or until it is steaming hot. Remove from the microwave and add the chocolate. Allow the chocolate and cream to rest for about 5 minutes before stirring, until the chocolate is fully melted and incorporated into the cream.

Fit another 16-inch (40-cm) piping bag with a round piping tip and fill halfway with the pastry cream. Pipe the pastry cream on half of the macarons shells, then top with the remaining shells. Dip one end of the macaron into the ganache. Leave them, ganache side up, on a wire rack until the ganache sets.

Best stored in an airtight container in the freezer for up to a month. Thaw in the refrigerator for 4 hours before serving.

Raspberry Cheesecake Macarons

YIELDS ABOUT 18 SANDWICH COOKIES

This recipe is great for testing your creativity and learning how to stretch the bounds of the delicate macaron shells by adding freeze-dried raspberries to the mix. You can use any freeze-dried fruit for a fun flavor change.

EQUIPMENT

Food processor

Medium-sized bowl

Fine-mesh strainer or sifter

Stand mixer with whisk attachment

Silicone spatula

3 rimmed baking sheets

Parchment paper or silicone baking mats

2-quart (2-L) saucepan

2 (16-inch [40-cm]) piping bags

Round piping tip

Small round tip

Toothpick

SHELLS

190 g powdered sugar

100 g ground almond flour

15 g freeze-dried raspberries

Lemon wedge, for cleaning equipment

120 g egg whites (from about 4 large eggs), left out overnight

⅛ tsp sea salt

40 g granulated sugar

1 to 2 drops pink gel food coloring (optional)

Make the macaron shells: In a food processor, combine the powdered sugar, almond flour and freeze-dried raspberries and pulse 10 to 15 times. Pour the mixture through a fine-mesh strainer or sifter into a medium-sized bowl. For the best results, you should sift the mixture a second time. Set aside.

Wash and dry your stand mixer bowl and whisk attachment. Gently rub with a slice of lemon and wipe dry again. This is to make sure there are no traces of fat on your equipment, which would prevent the egg whites from rising into a meringue.

Add the egg whites and salt. Beat the egg whites on medium speed until foamy, then slowly increase the speed to medium-high. Add the granulated sugar and beat until the mixture looks glossy and reaches stiff peaks. You can check whether the meringue has stiff peaks by removing the whisk from the mixer and dipping it into the meringue. Flip the whisk upside down: If the meringue points up, it is stiff; if it droops, it needs more mixing.

Mix in the food coloring. Add the almond flour mixture and use a silicone spatula to mix it into the meringue. Spread the mixture along the sides of the mixer bowl, then scrape it down and gently stir. You want to deflate the meringue and remove as much air as possible. Do this motion until your mixture moves around like lava. Test this by occasionally lifting up some of the batter and letting it drop down back into the bowl. It should drip down like a ribbon and then slowly incorporate back into the batter. If it just sits there or falls in clumps, mix longer.

Set aside for 30 minutes to allow any remaining air to leave the batter. Line three rimmed baking sheets with parchment paper or silicone baking mats.

Fit a round piping tip into a 16-inch (40-cm) piping bag and fill the bag halfway with the batter. Pipe rounds that are about 1½ inches (4 cm) wide and about 1 inch (2.5 cm) apart onto the prepared baking sheets. Refill the bag as needed, but always make sure it is never more than halfway filled.

Tap the baking sheets against your counter to help release any remaining air bubbles. Use a toothpick to pop any air bubbles that you see rise up. If there are any points from the piping, you can use a wet finger to press it down so the tops are flat.

(continued)

FILLING

½ cup (115 g) cream cheese, at room temperature

2 cups (240 g) powdered sugar

½ tsp vanilla extract

¼ tsp sea salt

⅓ cup (107 g) raspberry jam

¼ cup (25 g) graham cracker crumbs

Leave the sheets alone for at least 45 minutes to an hour, or until the tops are dry enough to touch without the batter sticking to your fingers. This is important to ensure you have smooth tops and develop proper feet.

Preheat the oven to 325°F (163°C) and bake one sheet at a time for 10 minutes, turning the sheet halfway through. Check that the macarons are ready to be removed by testing whether a macaron can be lifted off the baking sheet without breaking. Check every minute if the macarons are not ready after the first 10 minutes.

Remove from the oven and leave the macarons on the baking sheet for 5 minutes before transferring to a wire rack to cool completely. Bake the remaining macarons, one sheet at a time, and let cool completely.

Make the filling: In the stand mixer fitted with the paddle attachment, beat the cream cheese until smooth and creamy. Add the powdered sugar and beat until it fully incorporates. Beat in the vanilla and salt until fully combined.

Fit another piping bag with a small tip, and fill with the cream cheese mixture. Flip half of the macarons bottom up and pipe a ring all around just inside the edge, leaving a small hole in the center. Fill the center with the raspberry jam.

Sprinkle graham cracker crumbs over the cream cheese filling and raspberry jam. Top with the (right side up) remaining macaron shells.

Best stored in an airtight container in the freezer for up to a month. Thaw in the refrigerator for 4 hours before serving.

Swiss Macarons

Swiss macarons are my favorite type of macaron to make. They aren't as delicate as French macarons, but you are more likely to get consistently good results using this method. You don't have to worry about aging your egg whites, and they are so much more forgiving, so if it's a little more humid outside, you can still whip up a batch of these macarons. After mastering French macarons, I think it is nice to pull back a little and give you a method that isn't as temperamental.

Pink Lemonade Macarons

YIELDS 28 MACARONS

These macarons are bright and so much fun. They're a simple and tasty way to get you into making a Swiss macaron, since the shells are a basic vanilla. Instead, we infuse the cookies with flavor by using both frosting and lemon curd.

EQUIPMENT
Kitchen scale

3 or 4 rimmed baking sheets

3 or 4 silicone baking mats

Fine-mesh sieve or sifter

Medium-sized bowl

Heatproof stand mixer bowl

Balloon whisk

2-quart (2-L) saucepan

Stand mixer with whisk attachment

Silicone spatula

2 (16-inch [40-cm]) piping bags

Wide round piping tip

Round piping tip

Toothpick

SHELLS
100 g almond flour

100 g powdered sugar

100 g egg whites (from about 3 large eggs)

100 g granulated sugar

1 tsp vanilla extract

2 tsp (4 g) lemon zest

1 or 2 drops yellow gel food coloring

Line three or four rimmed baking sheets with silicone baking mats and set aside. Baking mats with macaron guides are highly encouraged.

Make the macaron shells: Using a fine-mesh sieve or sifter, sift the almond flour and powdered sugar into a medium-sized bowl, then set aside.

In a freshly washed and dried heatproof bowl of a stand mixer, using a balloon whisk, whisk together the egg whites and granulated sugar until they are just combined.

(continued)

Pink Lemonade Macarons (Continued)

Place the mixing bowl over a 2-quart (2-L]) saucepan filled with about 2 inches (5 cm) of simmering water. Heat over medium-low heat to prevent the water from boiling.

Whisk the mixture quickly and constantly, until the sugar is melted and the mixture is warm to the touch. Check this by dripping a drop of the mixture onto your pointer finger and rub with your thumb. You should not feel any granules from the sugar when it is ready. This process can take up to 10 to 12 minutes.

Return the bowl to your stand mixer, fitted with a freshly washed and dried whisk attachment. Turn the mixer speed to high and whisk the egg mixture until it forms a meringue with stiff peaks. Note: Check for stiff peaks by stopping the mixture and taking out the whisk attachment. Turn the whisk so the wires are pointing upward. If the meringue stuck to the whisk flops over easily, it is not ready. When the meringue sticks upright, with only the very tip of the meringue curling over, it is ready. This can take 10 to 15 minutes.

Add the vanilla, lemon zest and food coloring and whip until fully combined.

Sift the almond flour mixture on top of the meringue. Use a silicone spatula to slowly stir the dry ingredients into the meringue. Scrape the sides and bottom of the bowl to ensure all the meringue and dry ingredients are fully mixed in. Spread the mixture along the sides of your bowl and then scrape down into a pile. Repeat this a few times as you gently work the mixture. This helps remove excess air bubbles. You need to work slowly so as to not overmix, which will make your batter runny and unworkable.

Pull some of the batter and lift it up, if the batter runs down in a steady stream or ribbon, it is ready. Some people describe the batter as acting similarly to lava. If it plops down in bits, continue to mix for a few seconds at a time and check again and stop as soon as it reaches the ribbon texture.

Scoop some of the batter into a 16-inch (40-cm) piping bag fitted with a wide round tip. Do not overfill the bag, for the best control. It should be under the fill line if the bag has one. About one-third of the mixture will do well. Twist the top of the bag to close it off.

Pipe rounds that are about 1½ inches (4 cm) wide and about 1½ inches (4 cm) apart onto the prepared baking sheets.

Bang the baking sheets on the counter several times to release any air bubbles. Use a toothpick to pop any bubbles in the batter if you see them rise. If there are bumps on the top of the rounds from piping, use a moistened fingertip to gently smooth them down.

Let the macarons sit out until the tops are dry and a skin has formed. This can take anywhere from 15 to 45 minutes, depending on the weather, the heat of your kitchen, humidity, etc. You will know they are ready when you touch one with your finger and you can pull it away clean.

(continued)

Pink Lemonade Macarons (Continued)

FILLING

1½ oz (2 g) freeze-dried strawberries

½ cup (1 stick/114 g) unsalted butter, at room temperature

2 cups (240 g) powdered sugar

¼ tsp sea salt

½ tsp lemon juice

1½ tsp (8 ml) vanilla extract

3 to 4 tbsp (45 to 60 ml) heavy cream

⅓ cup (75 g) lemon curd

Preheat the oven to 290°F (143°C) and place a rack in the center. Bake the macarons, one sheet at a time, for 26 to 28 minutes, or until you can easily lift a macaron shell off the baking sheet. Remove from the oven and immediately remove the baking mat from the pan. Let the macarons cool completely before removing them from the mat. Bake the remaining macarons and let cool, one sheet at a time.

While the macarons cool, make the filling: In a food processor, process the freeze-dried strawberries until they become a fine powder.

In the bowl of your stand mixer fitted with the paddle attachment, beat the butter on medium speed until smooth. Add the powdered sugar, powdered strawberries and salt. Beat on low speed until the mixture comes together. The mixture may look lumpy, this is normal.

Add the lemon juice and vanilla, then slowly mix in the cream, 1 tablespoon (15 ml) at a time, until the frosting becomes smooth and spreadable.

Fit another second piping bag with a round tip, and fill with the frosting. Turn half of the macaron shells upside down and pipe a ring all around just inside the edge, leaving a small hole in the center. Fill the hole with lemon curd. Top with the remaining (upright) macarons.

Best stored in an airtight container in the freezer for up to a month. Thaw in the refrigerator for 4 hours before serving.

Chocolate Peanut Butter Macarons

YIELDS 28 MACARONS

One of my favorite memories growing up were the weekly movie nights with my sisters. We would all go to Blockbuster (wow, I'm really showing my age here), pick out movies and go home to make snacks. I am pretty sure that we made our own version of Muddy Buddies® (Puppy Chow® to some) pretty much every week. If you haven't had them before, muddy buddies are a peanut butter and chocolate-covered Chex® cereal that is then coated in powdered sugar. They're so delicious and a ton of fun in macaron form! These macarons are perfect because they bring together a few more advanced techniques to create something exciting to assemble, eat, and of course, share.

EQUIPMENT

Kitchen scale

3 or 4 rimmed baking sheets

3 or 4 silicone baking mats

Fine-mesh sieve or sifter

Medium-sized bowl

Heatproof stand mixer bowl

Balloon whisk

Stand mixer with whisk attachment

2-quart (2-L) saucepan

Silicone spatula

2 (16-inch [40-cm]) piping bags

Wide round piping tips

Toothpick

Microwave-safe bowl

Small saucepan

2 small bowls

Brush for coating

SHELLS

200 g almond flour

200 g powdered sugar

20 g unsweetened cocoa powder

200 g egg whites (from about 6 large eggs)

200 g granulated sugar

Line three or four rimmed baking sheets with silicone baking mats and set aside. Baking mats with macaron guides are highly encouraged.

Make the macaron shells: Using a fine-mesh sieve or sifter, sift the almond flour, powdered sugar and cocoa powder into a medium-sized bowl, then set aside.

In a freshly washed and dried heatproof bowl of a stand mixer, using a balloon whisk, whisk together the egg whites and granulated sugar until they are just combined.

Place the bowl over a 2-quart (2-L) saucepan filled with about 2 inches (5 cm) of simmering water. Heat over medium-low heat to prevent the water from boiling.

Whisk the mixture quickly and constantly (hello, arm workout!), until the sugar is melted and the mixture is warm to the touch. Check this by dripping a drop of the mixture onto your pointer finger and rubbing it with your thumb. You should not feel any granules from the sugar when it is ready. This process can take up to 10 to 12 minutes.

Return the bowl to your stand mixer, fitted with a freshly washed and dried whisk attachment. Turn the mixer speed to high and whisk the egg mixture until it forms a meringue with stiff peaks. Note: Check for stiff peaks by stopping the mixture and taking out the whisk attachment. Turn the whisk so the wires are pointing upward. If the meringue stuck to the whisk flops over easily, it is not ready. When the meringue sticks upright, with only the very tip of the meringue curling over, it is ready. This can take 10 to 15 minutes.

Sift the almond flour mixture on top of the meringue.

Use a silicone spatula to slowly stir in the dry ingredients into the meringue. Scrape the sides and bottom of the bowl to ensure all the meringue and dry ingredients are fully mixed in. Spread the mixture along the sides of your bowl and then scrape down into a pile. Repeat this a few times as you gently work the mixture. This helps remove excess air bubbles. You need to work slowly so as to not overmix, which will make your batter runny and unworkable.

(continued)

Chocolate Peanut Butter Macarons (Continued)

FILLING

8 oz (225 g) semisweet chocolate

½ cup (120 ml) heavy cream

⅓ cup (85 g) creamy peanut butter

COATING

¼ cup (50 g) granulated sugar

¼ cup (60 ml) water

1 cup (120 g) powdered sugar

Pull some of the batter and lift it up, if the batter runs down in a steady stream or ribbon, it is ready. Some people describe the batter as acting similarly to lava. If it plops down in bits, continue to mix for a few seconds at a time and check again and stop as soon as it reaches the ribbon texture.

Scoop some of the batter into a 16-inch (40-cm) piping bag fitted with a wide round tip. Do not overfill the bag for the best control. It should be under the fill line if the bag has one. About one-third of the mixture will do well. Twist the top of the bag to close it off. Pipe rounds that are about 1½ inches (4 cm) wide, about 1½ inches (4 cm) apart, onto the prepared baking sheets.

Bang the baking sheets on the counter several times to release any air bubbles. Use a toothpick to pop any bubbles in the batter if you see them rise. If there are bumps on the top of the rounds from piping, use a moistened fingertip to gently smooth them down.

Let the macarons sit out until the tops are dry and a skin has formed. This can take anywhere from 15 to 45 minutes, depending on the weather, the heat of your kitchen, humidity, etc. You will know they are ready when you touch one with your finger and you can pull it away clean.

Preheat the oven to 290°F (143°C) and place a rack in the center. Bake the macarons, one sheet at a time, for 26 to 28 minutes, or until you can easily lift a macaron shell off the baking sheet. Remove from the oven and immediately remove the baking mat from the pan. Let the macarons cool completely before removing them from the mat. Bake the remaining macarons and let cool, one sheet at a time.

While the macarons cool, make the filling: In a microwave-safe bowl, microwave the chocolate, cream and peanut butter, stirring every 30 seconds, until melted and smooth—60 to 90 seconds. Let the ganache set to a pipeable consistency. You can speed this up by putting it in the refrigerator; just stir it every 5 minutes, scraping the sides and bottom so it cools evenly.

Now, make the coating: In a small saucepan, combine the granulated sugar and water and stir to dissolve the sugar. Bring to a boil and boil for 30 seconds. Remove from the heat and transfer to a small bowl. Let cool to room temperature. Place the powdered sugar in another small bowl. Working a few shells at a time, brush the tops of each shell with the sugar mixture and let stand for 10 to 15 seconds, then toss in powdered sugar until coated.

Fit another 16-inch (40-cm) piping bag with a round piping tip, and fill with the cooled and set ganache. Turn half of the shells bottom up. Pipe a generous 1½ teaspoons (8 ml) of the ganache onto the shells, then sandwich together with the remaining (upright) shells.

Best stored in an airtight container in the freezer for up to a month. Thaw in the refrigerator for 4 hours before serving.

Macaron Troubleshooting

Everyone has a bad day when it comes to making macarons, but with some practice, you can understand what may or may not have gone wrong in the baking process. Here are some common issues and how to fix them!

Cracks: Cracks are the most common issue and can have many causes. The oven may be too hot or have hot spots. You can tell that the oven has hot spots if macarons on certain areas of the baking sheet consistently crack. The batter may also be undermixed. You may have air bubbles still in the batter due to undermixing or not tapping out the air bubbles before resting the piped macarons prior to baking.

Hollows: This can happen if the batter is overmixed or the meringue was overwhipped. You may also find this happens when the macarons are underbaked and the inside of the macaron begins to deflate as it cools.

No feet: There are many reasons that your macarons may not have developed feet. Your oven may not have been hot enough, or your batter was overmixed. The macarons may have rested too long or not long enough! This can also happen when there is too much liquid in the batter or the meringue was not beaten enough.

Feet too big: Big feet that protrude too much may happen if your oven is too hot or the batter was overmixed.

Bumpy tops: Bumpy tops will usually happen when you do not sufficiently process your almond flour and then sift out the larger pieces. This also happens when the batter is undermixed. There may have also been small air bubbles trapped in the batter.

Uneven shells: This typically happens when the batter was overmixed or not mixed well. This also sometimes happens when there are cold spots in your oven.

Batter overspreading: If the batter doesn't hold a nice circular shape or seems soupy, you may have overmixed your batter.

Wrinkly shells: This can happen when the meringue is overwhipped or when the batter is overmixed.

Shells stuck to the pan: Typically, this indicates that your macarons were underbaked.

Browned shells: Either the oven was too hot or the baking pan was too close to the heat source. You may also not be using the right food dye. Most dyes are not meant for baking and usually best for frostings and icings and may brown your macarons in the oven. Gel food colorings are easy to find and least likely to brown compared to liquid food colorings. Powdered food coloring is the best as it doesn't affect the batter consistency and won't accidentally brown in the oven.

Acknowledgments

First, I would like to thank my publisher, Page Street Publishing Co., and especially my editors, for believing in me and helping me bring this book to life.

I would also like to thank my family and friends for supporting me, cheering me on and giving me the confidence to keep moving forward not only with writing this book, but continuing to live life in Quinn's honor.

Thank you to my friends at Rodelle for being my vanilla lifeline as I tested and retested (and tested again) these recipes!

About the Author

Amanda started off as a self-taught baker. She had inspirations of being an expert baker while she learned how to make muffins, pies, and yes, cookies, for her flatmates in London to enjoy. After realizing her talent and passion for baking and sharing her creations, she decided to pursue it more academically and professionally. She is the founder of A Cookie Named Desire and has been featured online by many outlets, such as *The Today Show, America's Test Kitchen, Country Living*, Buzzfeed and even the clothing line Lane Bryant.

Index